Contents

Credits

For Mum and Dad

....

Acknowledgements

Many thanks to Mrs Lúcia Cooper for materials and guidance
and to Sarah Mitchell from Hodder for her total encouragement
in the first place. Thanks, also, to Ginny Catmur at Hodder, and
Rosemary Morlin for their work on this new edition. And to
Brazil, for instilling the fire of life. **Viva!**

Meet the author

I have had a connection with Portugal since living with a Portuguese family prior to starting my studies at Oxford in 1984. During my degree course I also spent a year in Brazil, an experience which I have drawn on frequently over the years in my teaching and writing. Since graduating with a degree in Portuguese and Spanish in 1988, I have also lived, worked and studied in Portugal, and continue to visit there each year with my family, often travelling through remote regions by public transport.

I have written a number of books on Portuguese language, life and culture, as well as on living, working and buying property there. I was invited to act as language consultant for the BBC's highly-acclaimed TV series 'Talk Portuguese', and have also given advice for the 'Brazil Inside Out' series.

I have been involved in Portuguese examinations in the UK since 1992, taking on the roles as Moderator for GCSE Speaking Tests, Principal Examiner for GCSE Writing, and Principal Moderator for Asset Speaking Tests; I was also the Subject Officer for Portuguese at the Awarding Body.

I continue to teach Portuguese language and culture in Lancaster and run the North-West Portuguese Circle. I am a keen and enthusiastic promoter of all things relating to the Portuguese-speaking world.

Sue Tyson-Ward

Only got a minute?

Portuguese is spoken by over 200 million people across the globe, with approximately 190 million of these in Brazil. Already an increasingly-important world economy, Brazil holds a wealth of diverse interests across a range of areas.

Portuguese has its roots predominantly in Latin, so if you already know languages such as French, Spanish, or Italian, you should be able to read Portuguese quite easily. If you have no prior knowledge of other languages, you need not worry; regular, short sessions of learning will help you overcome the basics quite quickly. Many words are also very similar to English, and spotting the links, unlocking the code, will give you the confidence and desire to keep up your learning. Complete Brazilian Portuguese is designed to do just that: to help you unlock the code of how the structure of Portuguese works, and to allow you the opportunity, at whatever level, to progress from repeating simple holiday phrases to creating your own sentences and saying what YOU want to say in response to what is happening around you.

Brazil is a place of inspiring landscapes, a wealth of culture, and friendly people, and is a wonderful place in which to try out the language: its laid-back approach to life cascades over into the way the language is manipulated. Even with just a few phrases under your belt, you will be so delighted with the response to your efforts that you will very easily want to go much further. Whether you want to be on the sun-drenched beaches of Rio, exploring the Amazon wonders, joining the Samba parades in February, or doing business in hi-tech São Paulo or Brasília, Brazilian Portuguese offers a great new world of opportunity. And should you take your learning to a higher level, you open the door to some fantastic Brazilian literature, song lyrics, films, and authentic recipes for amazing food. *Complete Brazilian Portuguese* gives you the possibility to do all of that with confidence.

Ride the crest of the wave into the Brazilian way of life, and become part of one of the world's most fascinating cultures.

5 Only got five minutes?

Why Brazilian Portuguese?

There are a number of very valid reasons why you might wish to take up Brazilian Portuguese:

▶ As a visitor to or potential resident in Brazil, for holiday purposes whilst there, or to get by more confidently dealing with the services and everyday life of your new environment.

▶ For business purposes: the world's eighth largest economy that is Brazil has much to offer foreign investors. More and more UK and US businesses are forging links there, and opportunities are constantly arising for interesting initiatives. Brazil continues to enjoy relative stability in its economy, which has engendered a lot of interest from foreign companies, financiers and investors alike.

▶ For adventure, eco-interests and voluntary work: the Amazon region of Brazil has long-been a magnet for anthropologists, linguists and ecologists, and in today's climate of global eco-concern, there is no better area for research. Brazil also offers many opportunities for voluntary work, from the densely-populated metropolis of São Paulo (with 17 million inhabitants, the world's third largest city), to the favela slums of Rio, and the large areas of the barren North-East.

▶ For educational purposes: there is huge scope for teachers of English in many parts of Brazil. There are a few good international schools mainly in Rio and São Paulo and hundreds, if not thousands, of English-language schools. And whilst English may be the language of function within the classroom, Portuguese will be your language of everyday life beyond. A number of British students have also spent fruitful study time at some of Brazil's universities, with particular links for business/management studies and ecologically-based areas of study.

If those reasons were not enough, you might be interested in world history and culture; Brazil's 'discovery' by Portuguese explorers back in 1500, and its subsequent development and break-away from Portuguese rule are a fascinating backdrop to this amazing country. You may have a love of world music, and from the mighty Samba and Bossa Nova to the 'Tropicalismo' movement of the 1960s and 1970s, and more modern musicians still beating out those mesmeric rhythms, what better way to use the language than understanding the lyrics of this music, and seeing straight into the soul of this diverse nation. Are you perhaps fascinated by world literature? What a world awaits you, in original writings from Brazil: the great Jorge Amado or Clarice Lispector, Machado de Assis, and the mystic Paulo Coelho. Have we mentioned the sport (**'futebol'** the obvious one), the food, the magnificent landscapes away from any trace of English speakers, the films (Brazilian cinema has produced some of the most acclaimed films in recent years)?

Or perhaps your interest lies in the pursuit of language for language-sake. And why not? Portuguese is a great choice, either for the novice language-learner or the already-accomplished linguist. It is basically a Romance (Latin-based) language, with a recognizable script (alphabet) and a not-too difficult sound system. It is described as a 'phonetic' language, that is in general terms what you see you pronounce. In this sense it is far easier than, say, French or English, both of which have complexities of spelling and sounds. It is also a very melodic language, and whilst the Portuguese of Brazil may sound very different from that spoken in Portugal, the recent spelling agreement (the new Acordo Ortográfico) between all the Portuguese-speaking countries, means that wherever you travel in the Lusophone world, there exists a consistency of how words are written. Each region will still maintain its own quirks of expression and vocabulary, in the same way as the English-speaking world.

Easing into the language

If you are new to languages, or a 'rusty' learner, you should not find (Brazilian) Portuguese too daunting. Forget any negative memories of old school languages, but try to draw on aspects of other languages you have been exposed to in the past – however distant or slight that may be. Links back to school French and Latin will help you recognize structures and vocabulary. Any experience of Spanish will be of particular help (although at times can also be a hindrance!).

Portuguese belongs to the group of languages named 'Romance' languages, based on Latin. It was also influenced over the years by Arabic (a legacy of its Moorish invaders), and to a much lesser extent, by some of the Celtic invaders. But it is predominantly Latin in structure and vocabulary. Its alphabet is the same as English, although the letters k, y and w are still mainly used in abbreviations, proper names or imported foreign words.

Due to its Latin roots, which are shared by many English roots, you will be heartened by the many words you can recognize, from your initial steps into Portuguese: **porto** (*port*), **papel** (*paper*), **serpente** (*snake*), **carro** (*car*). Verbs, on the other hand, pose more of an initial problem to English-speakers, as their endings change according to the person doing the action, and when. But it is a code you soon start to break.

The Portuguese world beyond Brazil

Let us not forget that the Portuguese-speaking family is actually a very important one in world terms. Portuguese is the official language of Portugal (including Madeira and the Azores), Brazil, Angola, Mozambique, Guinea Bissau, São Tomé and Príncipe, Cabo Verde, and is still an official language in some sections of society in Macau and in East Timor. It was also used in Goa and its influence, and testament to the far-flung edges reached by Portuguese navigators in the 15th and 16th centuries, can still be found in words such as vindaloo (**vinho** and **alho**, *wine* and *garlic* being the main ingredients of this Indian dish), marmalade (from **marmelo** – *quince*) and a good cup of char (from **chá**, or *chaa* introduced to the English courts by Catherine of Bragança, who married Charles II). Overall, in number-crunching terms, there are now well over 200 million native Portuguese speakers, either in their own countries, or living as immigrants in places such as the UK, France, Switzerland, Canada, South Africa and the USA. That places Portuguese as the sixth most widely spoken language in the world, far higher than French, German or Italian. It is the third most spoken European language in the world, behind English and Spanish. Learning Portuguese leads you into an amazing world with a fascinating and vitally important history, legacies of wonderful literature, cuisine, music and inventions, and a diversity of peoples.

Portuguese is a passport to great opportunities, and by learning Brazilian Portuguese, your success in and enjoyment of that hugely exciting mega-culture is yours for the taking!

10 Only got ten minutes?

Whatever reason your interest in Brazilian Portuguese may be – travel, tourism, business, cultural – you have chosen, or are about to choose, a vitally-important world language, the learning of which will open doorways into some of the world's most interesting culture. Portuguese is not only the language of the small country of Portugal, with its ten million inhabitants, but in fact the third most widely spoken European language in the world (behind only English and Spanish). There are now over 200 million native speakers of Portuguese spread around the globe. The language is the official means of communication in continental Portugal and the island groups of Madeira and the Azores, the five former African colonies of Angola, Mozambique, Guinea Bissau, São Tomé and Príncipe and Cabo Verde (Cape Verde). It also includes, of course, the 'giant' of South America, Brazil, on its own now accounting for around 190 million speakers. The language is also still spoken in East Timor and to a lesser extent, Macau. Overall, that places Portuguese as the sixth most widely spoken language in the world. And not a lot of people know that! What is definitely worthy of note is that UNESCO estimates that Portuguese has the highest growth potential as a language of international communication throughout South America and Southern Africa; alongside Spanish, it is already one of the fastest-growing languages of the west.

For many years, scholars of languages, history, literature and the Arts have been studying the cultures of these rich and diverse communities, but it is in more recent years that Portuguese has become a foreign language of choice for a much wider audience. Those wishing to use it on holiday, while travelling, for business purposes, or for the obvious enjoyment links to aspects of culture such as the amazing Brazilian music and film industry. And with Brazilian musicians, and writers such as the much-translated Paulo Coelho bringing the language to eminence on the world stage, Portuguese has increasingly grown in popularity as a beautiful language to learn, one that is fairly accessible and manageable at some level or other for most people.

In the English-speaking world, we have long suffered the illusion, set down by our colonizing forbears, that we can travel the globe with no knowledge of local language or customs, and still 'get by'. Well, yes, that is very true, and we can gesticulate, speak ever more loudly, and s-l-o-w-l-y, and the natives will somehow get over the dreadful hurdle of understanding us! It has to be said, too, that many educated Brazilians are very good at English (and Spanish), so we are oft lulled into a false cocoon of Englishness whilst visiting there; this, in turn, does little to engender the motivation to get stuck into learning the local language.

However, for vast amounts of this huge country you will not get very far without at least the very basics of Portuguese. Even in those areas seemingly developing themselves as potential tourist and property-investment spots, visitors have noted a real lack of English language skills amongst the everyday local people. However, for a relatively small investment of your time and effort in taking on board some Portuguese, you will always be rewarded with real value-added return: you will be exposed to the real country and its customs, and welcomed by its people.

You may, of course, need far more than the basics; more and more UK, US and world businesses have working links with Brazil; Brazil now forms part of what is termed the BRIC economies (those of Brazil, Russia, India and China – now considered the most important emerging world economies). Brazil represents an enormous canvas of opportunity for scientists, ecologists, sociologists, anthropologists, as well as for more ordinary 'ists' – tourists. It always has done, really, but now it has become far easier to get there, and recent developments in northern Brazil are encouraging more outsiders to invest in property there too. But for large expanses of this simply huge land-mass, a knowledge of Portuguese is absolutely vital. And that is where **Complete Brazilian Portuguese** comes in: supporting you to learn the structures of the language in order to enable you to form your own sentences and use the language for your own purposes and at your own level, as well as giving you handy phrases and cultural insights.

So, how did the language of such a small country emerge as such a global language heavyweight?

In order to understand how and why Portuguese is such a fundamentally important language, we need to look at how its history became part of the development of Brazil, which mapped out the pivotal role it came to play on the global stage.

To find out how it all began, let's first go back to the prehistoric times of Ancient Lusitânia. Portugal is one of the oldest nations in Europe, with a rich prehistoric culture still evident in large numbers of megalithic sites. The area was visited by various travelling cultures, such as the Phoenicians and Greek traders. In the 6th century BC the Carthaginians had control, then lost it to the Roman Empire, who called the Iberian peninsula 'Hispania Ulterior'. The most difficult of local tribes the Romans found lived north of Lisbon, and were known as the Lusitani, after whom the land had originally been named. The Romans, as elsewhere, left many signs of their time there, not only in buildings, but also in the language spoken by the invaders and their diverse legions of men. By the 5th century AD, invaders from the barbaric northern tribes had made their presence felt: Vandals, and Visigoths to name but two. But the southern invasions of Moors from northern Africa were to have a far longer and far-reaching impact on the territory, as they also did in neighbouring Spain. They arrived in 711, and stayed until the 13th century. They settled well and brought new farming methods, fruits and a relatively calm way of life. Linguistically, they also left some traces, though far less than the Romans before them. By the 8th century, Portugal was known as Portuscale and was ruled over by the king of Leon in Spain.

By the 12th century, Iberia had started its fight back against the Moors. In 1179 the Pope finally recognized a Portuguese kingdom, ruled over by Afonso Henriques, who successfully battled against the Moors in the 1139 Battle of Ourique. Throughout Europe the

Reconquest against the Moors was in full swing, having become the 'Western Crusade', and finally Portuguese territory was rid of its invaders and had its boundaries officially recognized by Castille in 1297 in the Treaty of Alcañices.

Over the next two centuries Portugal entered a period of immense activity which was to have a profound effect upon the rest of the world, as well as establish it as one of the world's leading lights in science, navigation, astronomy and geography. The era of explorations – the Discoveries – were initially sparked by a shortage of gold in Europe, together with the continuing idea of the Crusades. The Portuguese became masters of the map, creating their own style of boat, the **caravela**, and developing navigational equipment such as the compass. They were sponsored in much of their activities by Prince Henry (later called 'the Navigator' by English writers, although he never actually sailed himself). Many of the most famous navigators you may have heard of were of Portuguese provenance: Bartolomeu Dias rounding the Cape of Good Hope, Vasco da Gama reaching Calicut and opening up the routes to the East, the circumnavigation of the world by Ferdinand Magellan (yes, Portuguese, but in the service of Spain!), and the hugely important feat in 1500 of Pedro Álvares Cabral landing in Brazil.

Whilst this was, indeed, a momentous step in the history of both Portugal and Brazil, one cannot ignore the fact that the country had in fact been inhabited by indigenous peoples for as long as 50,000 years. Once the initial 'meet and greet' pleasantries had been carried out, and Cabral and his men had erected a cross in the name of Portugal, they sailed off in search of riches in Africa, and it was not until 1531 that Portuguese settlers properly arrived near the southern port of Santos. After that, the Portuguese king sent steady streams of settlers to form a mainstay of strength along Brazil's long coastline, in an attempt to ward off possible 'invasions' by other nationalities looking to exploit Brazil's resources. At that time, the most lucrative trading resource was the dye produced by an indigenous tree, known as the **'pau brazil'** (*brazilwood*). Later, it was sugar, then gold, that formed the basis of trade, but the name of the brazilwood tree remained as the country's new adopted name (although it was subsequently changed on a number of occasions). During the mid-1550s, Portuguese sugar traders were fully involved in the African slave trade, 'importing' millions to work on the plantations. They considered the Africans hardier workers, less likely to fall ill than the indigenous peoples. The vast majority ended up in northern Brazil, where the African influence of the people, their culture, religion and music is still very much in evidence today. Salvador, in the region of Bahia (northeastern Brazil) is still the heart of black Afro-Brazilian culture. The north-Brazilian religion known as **'candomblé'** (sometimes likened by outsiders to voodoo) was born at this time: the slaves had brought their own beliefs and gods with them to Brazil, but were subjugated by their Catholic masters; masked by Catholic names, their gods lived a dual-existence until finally slavery was abolished in 1888, and now there is open acceptance of these overseas influences. Many Brazilians, of all creeds and colours, throw flowers into the sea on New Year's Eve, to the goddess Iemanjá, and wear white in her honour.

Having established the settlements in the mid-15th century, Portugal then spent almost a hundred years defending its outposts against French, and then, more significantly, Dutch attack. The Dutch, in fact, were a successful operation, and took much of the northeast, particularly the state of Pernambuco. They were a huge presence in that part of Brazil for a good 30 years, until eventually driven back in a series of bloody encounters. Despite their withdrawal from Brazil, they, too, left their mark, and it is not unusual in northeastern Brazil to see blonde-hair and green eyes alongside the distinct black of African roots. As well as having to deal with outside invasions, the Portuguese in Brazil soon found themselves facing a threat from inside the country too, in the form of bands of roaming 'explorers' calling themselves **'bandeirantes'** after the flag-bearers leading their troops. In search of new territories, and ruthless in their pursuit of it, they massacred many thousands of indigenous people themselves. In the midst of this belligerence, two important markers in Brazilian history were laid down: the bandeirantes were responsible for pushing the limits of Brazilian territory westwards, gaining around 6 million square kilometres from the Spanish (who had made an agreement with the Portuguese back in 1494 to divide up the known world between them); it was also these marauding travellers who first 'found' gold, in the state of Minas Gerais, and in particular around the small town of Ouro Preto (*Black Gold*).

During the Napoleonic invasion of the Iberian peninsula during the 1800s, the Portuguese prince regent at the time, João VI, fled with his royal court, and took refuge in Rio. Liking his new-found territory so much, he declared himself ruler of the country, and on his accession to the Portuguese crown, he assumed kingship over Brazil too. It was in 1822 that Brazil finally became an empire liberated from the Portuguese crown, although ruled over by the prince regent Pedro, styling himself 'Emperor'. However, it was only when Pedro's young son, Pedro II, took over rule, that Brazil really started to prosper as an independent state. The 19th century saw the abolition of slavery, and the rise of the coffee bean as the new raw material to replace decreased exports of sugar. And by opening up its borders to allow foreigners in to work the coffee plantations, Brazil further expanded its melting pot of cultures that makes it one of the most interesting mixes of races today: Italians in their thousands, followed in subsequent decades by Japanese, Germans, Spanish and Chinese. There are huge Italian and Japanese communities in São Paulo, and Germanic influence is to be found in the south in towns such as Blumenau and its beer festivals. After the coffee 'rush' came the rubber, bringing great riches to the merchants of the Amazon region around Manaus, and Brazil's 'wealth' was sealed.

The following 50 or 60 years brought a series of dictators out of the woodwork, with brutal killings and 'disappearings' the salient features of their rules. Many outspoken, liberal thinkers were rounded up in the middle of the night and families were never reunited with loved ones. Many died incarcerated; others were summarily executed, and the fate of many others is simply still not known. It was not until the 1970s and 1980s that opposition to these regimes gathered momentum and confidence to act. By 1980, the newly-founded Workers Party **(partido dos trabalhadores)** had as its head one 'Lula' da Silva, an emblematic advocate of workers' rights – himself a one-time factory worker. Despite waves of relative stability, then crippling spiralling inflation of the intervening governments of leaders including José Sarney in the 1980s, then Fernando Collor de Mello and Henrique Cardoso, Lula and his party remained firm, and finally in 2002 was elected President, and re-elected in 2009. With vows to rid Brazil of its endemic corruption, crime and poverty, Lula da Silva has brought a breath of fresh air to Brazilian, and world, politics. However, his is an unenviable task of re-distributing the wealth of one of the world's largest economies: the vast majority of Brazil's riches still lie in the hands of a very small minority and those on the lowest rung of life are still battling to climb up, surviving through drugs and violence. No small task, then.

The language

Portuguese is mainly a Latin language, and as such, follows many patterns evident in other Romance languages you may be familiar with. Its verbs, for example, are fully conjugated (have different endings for each person), and words such as nouns and adjectives change their endings (there are masculine and feminine words). If you have a good knowledge of French, Spanish or Italian, you will have no problem in approaching Portuguese, especially the written language. The main differences between the two variants (European/African and Brazilian) of the language are the pronunciation of certain sounds, and vocabulary. Some grammatical structures are also slightly different. A new spelling agreement, long in the making, has just come into place, with the aim of standardizing spelling across the whole Portuguese world. But wherever you are in Luso-world, you can generally make yourself understood, whichever variant you speak. And Brazilians are definitely easier to listen to than their European cousins, as Brazilians open vowel sounds more and speak with colourful intonation, that it makes listening to them a real delight.

For those people reading this with no prior experience of learning a language, Portuguese also has many words which are very similar to English. There are certain patterns of endings, such as **-ção** which is the equivalent of -*tion* in English, such as in the words for *station* and *cooperation* – **estação** and **cooperação**. Portuguese uses the same alphabet as English and the same script, so there are no strange symbols to learn. Brazilians also incorporate many English words into their everyday speech, sometimes giving them their slant on pronunciation; the words 'shopping' (shopping centre) and 'short' (shorts) are commonplace. Portuguese is now the world's eighth most widely-used language on the Internet – it is a fully modern language with IT terminology, and even when you go back to some of its early writing, it is still fairly straightforward to read. It is the language of some fabulous literature, amazing Brazilian films, fantastic world music, and some of the most charming people you will meet anywhere. This publication, *Complete Brazilian Portuguese,* is designed to take you through the structures that form the language, from the most basic up to more complex ideas. Along the way, you will pick up the confidence to start putting together your own sentences, and you will quite quickly be able to recognize the way the language works by reading newspapers and magazines. Over time the structure of the language will become more familiar, and when you are next in Brazil, take the time to look at signs and notices, try to analyse adverts you see and snippets of conversations you hear – at cafés, in shops, at the station – the more you relate back to the building-blocks you have been studying, the more you'll learn!

Boa Sorte! *Good luck* and enjoy your Brazilian adventure.

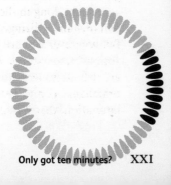

Personal introduction

Welcome to **Complete Brazilian Portuguese**. This course is designed
to increase your all-round basic knowledge of the structures of
Brazilian Portuguese, and how it all fits together in everyday
conversations and transactions. It also gives you a range of insights
into the way the language works, and handy tips on the culture
of Brazil. The course is based on the travels of a visitor to Brazil,
and as you accompany her trip around the vast country, you will
take on board useful everyday vocabulary, and aspects of Brazilian
life. During my teaching over the last 18 years, I have encountered
many learners who wish to go beyond the basics of learning a few
holiday phrases. However, many people were put off grammar at
school, and often say to me 'Do we have to learn any grammar in
this class?' My straight answer is always 'Yes, you do!' Without the
basic building-blocks of how a language works, you can never go
beyond learning phrases parrot-fashion. What happens next, when
your well-rehearsed phrase is answered in full and you, in turn,
cannot respond any further? This course is a steady mix of building
up the basic structures of the language alongside handy phrases
and interesting asides, and as such, aims to give you the freedom to
construct the sort of sentences you want to say yourself when you
are in Brazil. Created with beginners in mind, I have invested my
many years' experience of teaching and writing for adults into a
course dedicated to supporting your progress through the structure
of the Portuguese language, from a Brazilian perspective. You
can dip into the course, as and when you feel like it, or follow it
from start to finish. The more you work though the course, with
its built-in exercises, the more familiar you will become with how
Portuguese works, and the recordings allow you to hear authentic
Brazilian Portuguese at an even pace. Don't be afraid to have a go!
The course adheres to the most recent Portuguese Spelling Reform
currently being implemented across the Portuguese-speaking world.

Good luck – **Boa sorte!**
Sue Tyson-Ward

Introduction

This course is designed for the absolute beginner and requires no previous knowledge of any foreign language. The aim of the course is to enable you to use Brazilian Portuguese in everyday situations and also to provide some background information about Brazil and Brazilian culture.

The Portuguese of Brazil is different from that of Continental Portugal in three main ways: vocabulary, grammatical structures, and, most importantly, pronunciation. You could consider the two variants of the language in the same way as American and British English. It is widely considered that Brazilian Portuguese is actually easier to understand than European, as the Portuguese speak very quickly, with their mouths closed very much around the words, and they often 'eat' the beginning and ending of words. If you are learning Brazilian Portuguese, be assured that people will understand what you are saying (apart from the odd few words) throughout the Portuguese-speaking world. It is important for you to understand that you are learning not 'Brazilian', but 'Brazilian Portuguese'. It is surprising how many people (including some native speakers) believe 'Brazilian' is actually a language. It is not; it is a *variant* of the Portuguese language.

Portuguese is not a difficult language to take on board if you have had some experience of another Latin-based (or Romance) language, such as French, Spanish or Italian. Pronunciation is the main area you will need to concentrate on. Many people erroneously believe that, as it looks like Spanish, it will sound that way too. Constant practice with the recording will help you improve in this respect. If you have no knowledge of a Romance language, or in fact, of any language, take heart – you are starting out with a clean slate and with no preconceptions which could mislead you.

The American influence on Brazil, via TV and other mass-media communications has resulted in various English words entering the Brazilian speaker's vocabulary; words such as *shopping*, *flat* and *short* (*shorts*) are commonplace today.

How to use this book

Each of the 18 units is structured as follows:

Introduction. An introduction in English that explains what you will learn in the unit.

Dialogue. There are dialogues at the beginning of each chapter, and sometimes later on. Using the recording (where the symbol appears), listen to them first to check the pronunciation and see how much you understand, then read them carefully, and if necessary, listen again.

Vocabulary. The vocabulary section that follows each dialogue contains the new words and expressions that you will need to understand it.

True or false? These are statements about the texts in either English or Portuguese that may be true or false. The aim of these exercises is to check whether you have understood the text.

Cultural tips: Hints or tips – comments on life and society as well as background information on Brazil.

Test yourself. The important words and expressions used in the dialogues are repeated here, for you to test yourself. First, cover up the English and see if you can remember the meanings of the new Brazilian expressions. Once you can, try it the other way round, this time covering up the Brazilian.

Grammar. Notes explaining grammatical structures and how to create your own sentences.

Exercises/Practices. In these you practise the new words and information you have learnt.

Testing yourself – do you understand? Further dialogues and texts, testing your comprehension. These are not designed to test every word, but to give you the opportunity to 'get the gist' of a text.

The symbol ◀ᐧ) indicates material included on the accompanying recording.

The best way to make progress is to work a little every day. Listen to the recording and read the dialogues several times, learning the vocabulary before you start the exercises. Try to devise interesting ways to memorize the new words, such as through picture-images, songs, rhymes, etc.

Complete Brazilian Portuguese follows the journey of Sylvia Peters on a 6-month trip to Brazil, as she endeavours to make social, cultural and business links for future exchange. During the course of her journey you, like her, will visit some of Brazil's most important cities, and be introduced to its people, history and culture. Initially, Sylvia will be the guest of the Ferreira family; José is a marine biologist, and Marli teaches Portuguese in a language school. Sylvia returns to their house before leaving Brazil for the UK.

Glossary of grammatical terms

accents These are written marks above letters which affect either how that letter is pronounced, or at what point the word should be stressed (emphasized) when spoken. An accent can also be used to differentiate between two words with identical spellings but with different meanings. English does not use written accents (apart from on foreign words imported into the language), but many other languages do: e.g. *câmbio, fantástico; por = by/for pôr = to put.*

adjectives Words which describe, or give more information about, nouns. In Portuguese, adjectives match their endings to the nouns they are linked with (e.g. if they are singular/plural or masculine/feminine): e.g. *a cold cup of tea / that expensive coat* **um chá frio / aquele casaco caro.**

adverbs These are words which describe, or tell us more about, how an action (verb) is being carried out. They often answer the question HOW? They are also used to describe adjectives more fully, and you can use two adverbs together too. Often in English, an adverb has the ending '-ly' on it: e.g. *He sings loudly. / They ran incredibly quickly.* **Canta altamente. / Correram incrivelmente rapidamente.**

articles Words which go with nouns – definite articles are the words for 'the', and indefinite articles are the words for 'a/an/some'. In Portuguese there are different words corresponding to the number and gender (masculine/feminine): *o/a/os/as* (definite) and *um/uma/ uns/umas* (indefinite).

clause A group of words which also contains a verb: e.g. before *we go out ... / if she swims well ...* **antes de sairmos ... / se ela nadar bem ...**

comparative Forms of adjectives and adverbs used to make comparisons, e.g. *fatter / more slowly* **mais gordo / mais devagar.**

demonstratives The words used for pointing things out – *this / that / these / those* **este / esse / aquele / estes** etc.

. . . .

imperative A form of verb, known as a mood, used when giving commands: *Eat your dinner!* **Come o jantar!**

. . . .

infinitive The part of the verb referred to in English as 'to …', and the form found in the dictionary before you change any of its endings: *to speak / to drink / to leave* **falar / beber / partir**.

. . . .

interrogatives Question forms, e.g. *where? / which?* **onde? / qual?**

. . . .

nouns A noun is any thing, person or abstract idea in existence – everything around us is a noun of some kind. A noun can be singular (just one), or plural (more than one). In Portuguese, nouns are also divided into masculine and feminine words: e.g. *table / horses / man–men / happiness* **mesa / cavalos / homem–homens / felicidade**.

. . . .

number Whether a word is singular (just one), or plural (more than one).

. . . .

object The person or thing on the receiving end of the action of a verb. Objects can be 'direct' – i.e. they dirctly receive the action of the verb – or 'indirect' – where they receive the results of the action, through indirect means: e.g. *She gives money every week* ('money' is direct object) / *she gives them money every week.* ('them' is indirect object) **Dá dinheiro todas as semanas. / Dá-lhes dinheiro …** .

. . . .

phrase A group of words which together have some meaning: e.g. *in the square / after mid-day* **na praça / depois de meio-dia**.

. . . .

possessives Words showing ownership or possession, e.g. *my car / it's ours* **o meu carro / é nosso**.

. . . .

prefix A number of letters which may be added to the beginning of a word, which change its meaning in some way: e.g. *possible – impossible* / **possível – impossível**.

prepositions These are words which denote the 'position' of someone or something in time or place: e.g. *on top of the cupboard / before going out / at six o'clock* **em cima do armário** / *antes de sair* / *às seis horas.*

pronouns These are words which take the place of a noun (pro = for), so that you do not need to keep repeating the actual noun itself each time you want to refer to it. There are various types of pronoun, all of which you will learn about in Portuguese: e.g. **Maria** *is very kind.* **She** *looks after my cat.* **She** *gives* **it** *lots of treats.* **(A) Maria** / **Ela** / **-lhe.**

reflexive verbs Actions with a bearing on the subject of the verb – actions are carried out by, and also on, the subject, i.e. they 'reflect' back to the person carrying out the action. In English reflexive verbs carry the word 'self' with them. A number of verbs in Portuguese are reflexive where you would not expect them to be in English: e.g. *Enjoy* **yourselves!** / *She gets* **herself** *dressed each morning.* **Divertam-se!** / **Veste-se cada manhã.**

sentence A group of words, with a beginning, an end, and a finite verb (see below), which has a meaning. A sentence may have any number of separate clauses, but one of these will be the main clause, which can make sense in its own right as a sentence: e.g. *She wants to visit America. / If you go there, you should not drink the water.* **Ela quer visitar os Estados Unidos.** / **Se for lá, não deveria beber a água.**

subject The person or thing carrying out the action of a verb: e.g. *My brother wants to be a teacher. / Our dog always chases spiders.* **O meu irmão ...** / **O nosso cachorro ...**

subjunctive mood A separate set of verb endings for use in certain situations, such as in 'if' clauses, or with expressions of doubt: e.g. *I doubt he's coming* **Duvido que ele venha.**

suffix A number of letters which may be added to the end of a word, which change the meaning or the type of grammatical word it is: e.g. *sad – sadness / glad – gladly* **triste – tristeza** / **feliz – felizmente.**

superlative The form of an adjective or adverb denoting the highest or lowest level, e.g. *the fastest car / the cheapest shoes o carro mais rápido / os sapatos mais baratos.*

syllable This is a part of a word containing one, two, or more letters which are clumped together so that we can divide up the word as we say it: e.g. *cho-co-late / mag-ni-fi-cent cho-co-la-te / mag-ní-fi-co.*

tenses These are the time references for when verbs are taking place. There are different tenses in the present, past and future – you will learn what these are in Portuguese. Some of them have different names in Portuguese grammar from what they might be termed in English – don't worry too much about the actual terminology; concentrate on learning which verb endings to use in what circumstances: e.g. *She had not wanted to go to the party. / Will we have saved enough money? Não tinha querido ir à festa. / Teremos poupado dinheiro suficiente?*

verbs Verbs convey actions or states of being, or sometimes abstract states. Verbs have an 'infinitive' form, which tells you the name of the verb itself, but no other information – it is the form you will find in the dictionary, and relates to the English 'TO do something'. A sentence must have a verb in a 'finite' form – which tells you what the action is, who is doing it, and at what point in time (in the past, present or future). English does not change many of its verb endings, but Portuguese, as many languages, has different endings for the person doing the action, and the time, or tense: e.g. *She goes home at 5 o'clock. / I watched TV last night. Ela volta para casa às cinco. / Vi a televisão ontem à noite.*

Pronunciation

◀) CD1, TR 1, 01:10

Although this book can successfully be used on its own, the
purchase of the recording will enhance both your pronunciation
and your comprehension abilities as well as giving you the
opportunity for aural revision.

In native Portuguese words there is no **k**, **w**, or **y**, although they
appear in imported words. Pronunciation in Brazil varies from region
to region, as it may do in any country. There are certain distinct
sounds in Rio which mark the speaker as a 'Carioca' (a native of Rio),
e.g. the **de** sound at the end of a word pronounced as **gee**.

The whole Portuguese alphabet is as follows. If you have the
recording, listen to how it sounds when recited in Portuguese.

a b c d e f g h i j (k) l m n o p q r s t u v (w) x (y) z

Portuguese vowels

Portuguese vowel sounds are tricky to imitate, as there are nasal
sounds, and sounds differ depending on where the vowel is in
any given word. However, Brazilians do open their mouths wider
than the Portuguese, and are therefore theoretically easier to
understand! Here is a general idea:

a, as in *rather* – **falar**   or as in *abide* – **mesa**
ã, as in *rang* – **irmã**.   This is a nasal sound.
e, as in *bell* – **certo**   or as in *madden* – **pesar**
i, as in *mean* – **partida**   or as in *cigar* – **emigrar**
o, as in *saw* – **nova**   or as in *boot* – **sapato**
u, as in *boot* – **durmo**   or as in *bull* – **mudar**

Portuguese consonants

Portuguese consonants also differ from the English sounds in different situations. Follow the table on the recording, if you have it, as each consonant is given an English equivalent, and a Portuguese example:

Consonant	English sound	Portuguese sound
b	*ball*	bonito
c + e/i, ç	*sat*	cem, começa
c + a/o/u	*can*	comer
ch	*shout*	chocolate
d	*dab/'gee'*	dar or cida**de**
f	*fun*	falar
g + e/i	*pleasure*	geléia
g + a/o/u	*got*	pagar
h	*'silent'*	hotel
j	*pleasure*	julho
l	*last*	livre
lh	*billion*	mulher
m	*map*	mesa
n	*nod*	nadar
nh	*onion*	vinho
p	*pin*	parar
q(u)	*quart*	quando
q(u) + e/i	*'silent u'*	quem
r (initial)	*'aspirated'*	rio
r	*ran*	compram
s	*sat*	sol
s + vowels	*zoo*	casa
t	*tap*	todo
v	*'as in English'*	vida
x	*shout*	baixa
z	*zoo*	fazer

Spelling

Portuguese uses the Roman alphabet, as do English and other Latin-based languages. However, the letters **k**, **w** and **y** do not naturally occur in Portuguese words – only in imported foreign words and in abbreviations for weights, measures and chemicals, e.g. 10 kg (= 10 **quilos**). However, they have now been accepted into the official alphabet.

▶ The only double consonants you will find are **rr** and **ss**, which both change the sound from the single letter, plus **cc**, **mm** and **nn** (all less common).

▶ There are three extra 'sounds' or letter combinations you will come across a lot: **ch**, **lh**, **nh**. They are known as *diágrafos* – two letters with one sound. For readers with a background in Spanish, **lh** is similar in sound to Spanish *ll*, and **nh** is like *ñ*. **ch** is pronounced *sh* and not *ch* as in Spanish.

▶ **h** is always silent in Portuguese, thus sometimes making it difficult when listening to discern whether a word begins with a vowel or an **h**. As any dictionary will illustrate, there are in fact a number of words starting with h, so learning obvious ones will help – and many are similar to English so you can train yourself to think logically when listening, e.g. **o Otel Miramar** or **o Hotel Miramar**?

▶ A quick note about the consonants **c**, **g** and **q**, which change their pronunciation depending on which vowels follow them. This can be a stumbling block for the uninitiated, hence some basic rules here:

c before a / o / u = hard sound, like cat
ç (c + cedilla – see section on accents) before a / o / u = soft sound, like face
c before e / i = soft, like face
g before e / i = soft, like the s sound in treasure

g before a / o / u = hard, like in **g**oal

g + u before e / i = 'silent' u, e.g. **g**uitarra [ghee... not gwee...].

There are some exceptions (there always are!), such as **linguiça** (spicy sausage) [lingwiça].

q is always followed by **u**.

qu before e / i = 'silent' u, e.g. máquina (*machine*) [mákeena not mákweena]; again there are some exceptions (e.g. cinquenta (*fifty*) [cinkwenta]).

qu before o / a = kw, e.g. **q**uadro (picture) [kwadro]

▸ **ph** does not exist in Portuguese; those words similar to English have an **f** – the same sound, but be careful with the spelling: e.g. filósofo = *philosopher*.

Brazilian spelling

After many years of wrangling over spelling throughout the Portuguese-speaking world (and most particularly between Portugal and Brazil), up-to-date orthographic (spelling) agreements have now been agreed under the new Acordo Ortográfico. There are still some differences in spelling between the two main variants of the language, Brazilian and Luso-African, which includes those African countries with Portuguese as an official language.

Changes that have been agreed will still take a number of years to implement in all written material. This current edition of **Complete Brazilian Portuguese** complies with the new Acordo.

Punctuation / Pontuação

Just for reference, here are the names of some of the more common features of punctuation – they are useful in dictation!

.	ponto final	!	ponto de exclamação
,	vírgula	...	reticências
;	ponto e vírgula	«...» or "..."	aspas / vírgulas altas (comas)
:	dois pontos	( )	parênteses
?	ponto de interrogação	–	travessão

Students of Spanish should note that Portuguese does not have an upside-down ? or ! at the start of sentences.

Accents

You will find the following written accents in Portuguese:

´	acute accent	acento agudo	opens vowel sound and indicates stress*	gramática
^	circumflex	circunflexo	closes vowel sound and indicates stress	português
~	tilde	til	nasalizes vowel and usually indicates stress	amanhã
`	grave accent	acento grave	opens vowel, non-stressing, indicates a contraction of two words: preposition **a** and feminine forms of the definite article and the demonstrative pronouns and adjectives	àquele

*Stress is the part of the word you emphasize when you say it.

There are also: ç, *c-cedilla* (**cedilha**), which makes the c soft, and the 'dieresis' (trema), ü, in words of foreign origin, such as **mülleriano** (*Müller-like*).

Stress

Portuguese words are classified into three groups in terms of where the stress (emphasis) falls:

1 = last syllable
2 = penultimate (next to last) syllable
3 = antepenultimate syllable

The majority belong to group 2 and do not usually require a written accent. The written accent occurs to enable words to be correctly stressed when they have deviated from the usual stress pattern. Whenever you see a written accent, that is where you should emphasize the word when you say it. Words also carry a written stress mark to distinguish them from a word with the same spelling but a different meaning, e.g. **por** (*by*) and **pôr** (*to put*).

The above is a very basic guide to the concept of stress; for a fuller treatment of all the rules refer to the pronunciation guides in courses and dictionaries, and listen to how words are said when you are in Brazil. The best way to learn how to write the words correctly, though, is by practice, and that includes reading in the language and spotting spellings, as well as noting down new words as you acquire them. So, on with the rest of the book to do just that …

A few tips to help you acquire an authentic accent

It is not absolutely vital to acquire a perfect accent. The aim is to be understood; here are a number of techniques for working on your pronunciation:

1 Listen carefully to the recording or a native speaker or teacher. Whenever possible repeat aloud imagining you are a native speaker of Portuguese.
2 Record yourself and compare your pronunciation with that of a native speaker.
3 Ask native speakers to listen to your pronunciation and tell you how to improve it.
4 Ask native speakers how a specific sound is formed. Watch them and practise at home in front of a mirror.

Make a list of words that give you pronunciation trouble and practise them.

Seu passaporte, por favor
Your passport, please

In this unit you will learn
* *How to identify people*
* *How to introduce yourself and address people*
* *How to say hello and goodbye*
* *How to check into your hotel*

Dialogue 1

Sylvia Peters arrives in Brazil and passes through Customs (**Alfândega**).

Inspetor	Bom dia. Seu passaporte, por favor.
Sylvia	Aqui está.
Inspetor	Você é inglesa, não é?
Sylvia	Sim, sou.
Inspetor	Muito bem. Quanto tempo vai passar aqui?
Sylvia	Seis meses.
Inspetor	Está bem. Obrigado. Tchau.
Sylvia	Bom dia, obrigada.

 CD1, TR 2, 00:11

QV

bom dia *hello, good morning (also goodbye)*
aqui, cá *here*
está *(it) is*

seu *your*
você *you*
passaporte (o) *passport*
é *is/are*
por favor *please*
inglesa *English (woman)*
não é? *isn't it/is that so?*
tempo (o) *time*
não *no, not*
seis *six*
sim *yes*
meses (os) *months*
sou *I am*
está bem *OK*
muito bem *very well*
obrigado/a *thank you*
vai passar *you're going to spend*
tchau *see you/bye*
quanto? *how much?*

True or false?

Tick true (*verdadeiro*) or false (*falso*) for the following statements based on the dialogue.

V   F

a Sylvia Peters is American.
b She's going to spend six weeks in Brazil.
c She arrives in the morning.

Grammar

To be

In Portuguese there are two verbs both meaning **to be**:

Ser is used for permanent characteristics, such as nationality. **Estar** is used more for temporary states and locations.

In the dialogue you saw examples of both verbs:

aqui está	*here it is*	**estar**
você é inglesa	*you are English*	**ser**
sim, sou	*yes, I am*	**ser**
está bem	*that's OK*	**estar**

You will come across more examples, and find out other ways in which the verbs are used, as you work through the units.

Forms of address: **você**

In Brazil, most people call each other *you* using the word **você**. However, there are certain situations where more, or less, formality in address is called for. Look at the table below to see how these differences work.

Situation	Formal 'you'	Informal 'you'
With strangers, people in higher social/work position	**o senhor** (to man) **a senhora** (to woman)	
With friends, colleagues, family		**você/tu** (some parts of Brazil)
With older people	**o senhor/a senhora**	

Você and **tu** are examples of what are called *personal pronouns* – the words for *I*, *you*, *he*, etc.

Personal pronouns

The Portuguese personal pronouns are used to denote which person is carrying out the action of a verb. They are:

eu	*I*		**nós**	*we*
(tu)	*you* [used only in some parts of Brazil]			
ele	*he/it*		**eles**	*they* (male)
ela	*she/it*		**elas**	*they* (female)
você	*you*		**vocês**	*you* (plural)

These are referred to as *subject pronouns*, but they are not necessarily used all the time; in many instances the endings of the verbs will suffice to tell you who is doing the action. In the dialogue you had:

é inglesa *you are English*
sim, sou *yes, I am*

You will learn more of verbs later on.

Male/female

In Portuguese, everything you see around you is divided into two groups: masculine and feminine. This is because Portuguese is a language with its roots in Latin, and the Romans used a language system based on words linking together, usually in a logical way (although it may not seem so to many learners!). So, for example, *table* happens to be a feminine word, and *floor* is a masculine one. In most cases you can tell which group a word belongs to by its ending: an -o for masculine words, and an -a for feminine ones, although this is not always the case. A dictionary will guide you when you are first learning, and look for help in the vocabulary lists, until you start to get a feel for the different endings. In our vocabulary boxes, we have used o/a and their plurals os/as to show you what 'gender' a word is.

Obrigado/a

You will have noticed in the dialogue that the Customs official says **Obrigado**, and Sylvia replies **Obrigada**, both meaning *Thank you*. All men should use the first and women the second, regardless of whom they are addressing. This is because **Obrigado** is an adjective – a word of description, which is applied to the person expressing their gratitude – as in the outdated English (*I am*) *much obliged*. Another adjective you came across was **inglesa** (*English woman*). The masculine is **inglês** (*English man*). More on nationalities in Unit 2.

Dialogue 2

Sylvia arrives and checks in at the hotel where she will be staying before going to the Ferreira home.

Sylvia	Boa tarde. Sou Sylvia Peters. Tem um apartamento reservado em meu nome?
Rececionista	Um momento. Como se escreve seu sobrenome?
Sylvia	P-e-t-e-r-s. Peters.
Rececionista	Ah, sim, aqui está. A senhora Peters, de Manchester.
Sylvia	Isso.
Rececionista	Um apartamento com banheiro para três dias, sim?
Sylvia	Sim.
Rececionista	É o apartamento número quinze, no primeiro andar. Aqui tem a chave.
Sylvia	Muito obrigada.
Rececionista	De nada.

boa tarde *hello, good afternoon*
tem? *do you have?*
apartamento (o) *hotel room*
reservado *reserved*
em meu nome *in my name*
um momento *just a second*
como se escreve? *how do you write it?*
sobrenome (o) *surname*
de *of, from*
isso *that's it*
com *with*
banheiro (o) *bathroom*
para *for*
três *three*
dias (os) *days*
número (o) *number*

quinze *fifteen*
no primeiro andar *on the first floor*
chave (a) *key*
muito obrigada *thanks very much*
de nada *don't mention it*

Exercise 1

Tick **a** or **b** to complete the following statements.

1 Sylvia Peters is from	**a**	London	**b**	Manchester
2 She's going to stay	**a**	8 days	**b**	3 days
3 Her room number is	**a**	15	**b**	12

Grammar

A, an

The Portuguese words for *a (an)* are:

um (used with masculine words) **um apartamento** *a room*
uma (used with feminine words) **uma chave** *a key*

With more than one (i.e., in the plural), the words become:

uns (used with masculine plural words)
   uns apartamentos *some rooms*

umas (used with feminine plural words)
   umas chaves *some keys*

The

Similarly, Portuguese has four words to convey the English word *the*:

o *masculine singular* **o apartamento** *the room*
a *feminine singular* **a chave** *the key*

os   *masculine plural*   os apartamentos   *the rooms*
as   *feminine plural*   as chaves   *the keys*

Plural nouns

When you have more than one item (noun), the basic way to form the plural is to add an -s, as in the examples above:

o apartamento   os apartamentos
a chave   as chaves

Beware of irregularities, which abound in Portuguese, such as o mês (*month*)   os meses (*months*).

Numbers

◀ **CD1, TR 2, 02:14**

Here are the numbers 0 to 20, some of which have appeared in the first two dialogues.

0	zero		
1	um, uma	**11**	onze
2	dois, duas	**12**	doze
3	três	**13**	treze
4	quatro	**14**	catorze (quatorze)
5	cinco	**15**	quinze
6	seis	**16**	dezesseis
7	sete	**17**	dezessete
8	oito	**18**	dezoito
9	nove	**19**	dezenove
10	dez	**20**	vinte

Numbers *one* and *two* have both a masculine and a feminine form, so if you are talking about two houses, it's **duas casas**.

Dialogue 3

Sylvia pops out in the evening to meet up with the Ferreiras. She knows José but has not yet met Mrs Ferreira.

CD1, TR 2, 02:52

José	Boa noite, Sylvia, tudo bem?
Sylvia	Oi, José, tudo bem.
José	Sylvia, esta é minha mulher Marli.
Sylvia	Muito prazer.
Marli	Igualmente. Bem-vinda a São Paulo. Como está?
Sylvia	Bem, obrigada.
José	Bom, vamos sentar? Que vão tomar?

QUICK VOCAB

boa noite *hello, good evening/night*
tudo bem(?) *everything OK(?)*
oi *Hi*
esta *(f) this*
minha mulher *my wife*
muito prazer *pleased to meet you*
igualmente *likewise*
bem-vinda a São Paulo *welcome to São Paulo*
bom *right then*
vamos *shall we/let's*
sentar *to sit down*
que vão tomar? *what are you going to have (to drink)?*

Exercise 2

Can you fill in the missing words from these statements?

a _____ noite. Tudo _____?
b Esta _____ minha mulher.
c _____ prazer.

Grammar

This, these

When identifying people, or things, or when pointing them out, the words for *this* (*these*) are:

este (masculine person/thing) *this* **esta** (feminine person/thing) *this*
estes (masculine plural) *these* **estas** (feminine plural) *these*

este apartamento *this room*   **estes apartamentos** *these rooms*
esta chave *this key*   **estas chaves** *these keys*

Possession: my, your, etc.

In the dialogues you were introduced to some of the possessive words: **seu** *your*, **minha** *my*. Here is the full table for *my* and *your*:

	Singular		Plural	
	masculine	feminine	masculine	feminine
my	**meu**	**minha**	**meus**	**minhas**
your	**seu**	**sua**	**seus**	**suas**

The possessive word links to the item being possessed, and NOT the person to whom it belongs; therefore to say *my key*, you need to know that key is a feminine word; then choose **minha** from the table; **minha chave** = *my key*. Similarly, to say *your rooms*, you need to know that *room* is a masculine word, and it is in the plural, hence **seus apartamentos**. You will learn more possessives as you progress. Note that sometimes you will hear (or see) the possessive forms expressed as, for example: **A sua chave; OS seus apartamentos**; with the appropriate word for *the* going with the possessed item.

(O) meu passaporte *my passport*   **(AS) suas chaves** *your keys*

Questions, questions

To ask basic questions in Portuguese, all you have to do is raise your voice in a questioning tone at the end of a statement: **Tudo bem,** *OK.* **Tudo bem?** *OK?*

You can also 'tag' question-phrases on to statements, e.g. **Você é inglesa, não é?** *You're English, aren't you?* **Um apartamento para três dias, sim?** *A room for three days, yes?*

There are also question-words, known as interrogatives, with which you can begin a question. So far you have met:

Quanto? *How much?*   **Como?** *How?*   **Que?** *What?*

Test yourself

bom dia	*hello/good morning/goodbye*
boa tarde	*hello/good afternoon/goodbye*
boa noite	*hello/good evening/goodnight*
oi	*hi/hello*
tudo bem?	*how are things?/everything OK?*
como está?	*how are you?*
tudo bem	*fine/OK*
bem obrigado/a	*well, thanks*
tchau	*see you/bye*
muito prazer	*pleased to meet you*

> ## Insight
> ### Greeting people
>
> Brazilians are very tactile, open, friendly people, and it is common for them to kiss each other on greeting and saying goodbye. Men often shake hands with each other. Take your cue from their behaviour towards you and those around you.

Insight

Brazilian police

Brazilian police at airports, border patrols, and in general, are not to be messed about with! Make sure you have all your documentation in order (passport, visa, travel documents, driving licence, addresses of where you are staying). It is not unheard of for police to routinely check your vehicle and, inevitably, find something wrong with it. Often they are looking for a bribe, but you must be very careful here, as some travellers proffering money inside their passport have then been fined for so doing! The best policy, in many cases, is to keep quiet and pay the fine.

Practice

1 Now see if you can do the following:

a say *good morning, good afternoon, good evening*

b say *thank you, goodbye* (casually)

c say who you are

d ask if there is a room reserved in your name

e say *Hi, how are things?*

2 Give your part of the dialogue at the airport.

Inspetor	Boa tarde. Seu passaporte por favor.
You	*(Say here it is.)*
Inspetor	Você é inglês/inglesa?
You	*(Say yes I am.)*
Inspetor	Vai passar quanto tempo aqui?
You	*(Say eight days.)*
Inspetor	Muito bem. Tchau.
You	*(Say goodbye.)*

3 Work out the answers to these sums and write them out in words in Portuguese.

a dois e (and) cinco   =

b oito e seis   =

c dezenove menos (minus) dois =

d um e dez =

e vinte menos sete =

◀) CD1, TR 2, 03:52

4 Look at the Bingo card below, and listen for your numbers being called out on the tape. Cross off any you hear, then write out in words in Portuguese the two you are left with.

12	3	18
6	10	9

5 Look at the pictures and link them to what people are saying.

i boa noite

ii bom dia

iii tchau

iv muito prazer

v boa tarde

◀) CD1, TR 2, 04:30

6 Listen to the dialogue in the hotel, and tick the appropriate answers to the questions.

    a What is the man's name?   John Harris ☐   John Peters ☐

    b Where is he from?   London ☐   Liverpool ☐

    c How long is he staying?   6 months ☐   6 days ☐

    d What is his room number?   12 ☐   2 ☐

Testing yourself – do you understand?

Look at the following hotel booking-in form, and answer the questions that follow.

HOTEL SÃO LUÍS	
NOME:	*Senhor T. Andrews*
LUGAR DE ORIGEM:	*Londres*
Nº DE DIAS:	*Seis*
TIPO DE APTº:	*Com banheiro*
Nº DE APTº:	*treze*

1 Is the guest male or female?
2 S/he is from Italy. True or false?
3 S/he is staying six days. True or false?
4 What type of room has s/he got?
5 S/he is in room no. 12. True or false?

2

Você é casada?
Are you married?

In this unit you will learn
- *How to talk about yourself and your family*
- *How to talk about your home town*
- *How to give your address and telephone number*

Dialogue 1

Sylvia and the Ferreiras are sitting in a cafe in São Paulo. They are getting to know each other a bit better. The waiter (**o garçom**) brings their order.

◉ CD1, TR 3, 00:10

Garçom	Vamos ver. Um chope para o senhor Ferreira, um cafezinho para a senhora Ferreira, e um vinho tinto para a senhora.
José	Obrigado.
Marli	Você é de Manchester, não é?
Sylvia	Sim, sou.
Marli	E como é a cidade de Manchester?
Sylvia	Bem, é grande e muito movimentada.
Marli	Sylvia, você é casada? Tem filhos?
Sylvia	Sim, tenho dois, um filho e uma filha.
Marli	Como eles se chamam?

Sylvia	Meu filho se chama Robert. Ele tem dezesseis anos e é estudante. Minha filha se chama Clare, tem vinte e três anos e é casada.
Marli	E seu marido? Qual é o nome dele?
Sylvia	Meu marido se chama Tony e ele trabalha numa empresa internacional que fabrica produtos químicos. E você, Marli, trabalha?
Marli	Sim, sou professora de português numa escola de línguas. E você?
Sylvia	Eu também trabalho – para uma empresa interessante; sou advogada.

vamos ver *let's see*
um chope *a draught lager*
cafezinho (o) *espresso coffee*
vinho tinto (o) *red wine*
como é ...? *what's ... like?*
cidade (a) *city/town*
grande *large*
movimentado *busy*
casada *married*
filhos (os) *children*
tenho *I have*
filho (o) *son*
filha (a) *daughter*
como eles se chamam? *what are they called?*
se chama *is called*
ele/ela tem ... anos *he/she is ... years old*
vinte e três *23*
estudante (o/a) *student*
marido *husband*
qual é o nome (dele)? *what is (his) name?*
trabalha *work(s)*
numa empresa *in a company*
que *that, which*
fabrica *makes/produces*
produtos químicos (os) *chemicals*

professora (a) *teacher*
português *Portuguese*
numa escola *in a school*
línguas (as) *languages*
também trabalho *I also work*
internacional *international*
interessante *interesting*
advogada (a) *lawyer*

True or false?

Say if these statements are **verdadeiro** or **falso**.

		V	**F**
a	Sylvia is having beer.		
b	Sylvia has three children.		
c	Sylvia's daughter is married.		
d	Marli is a maths teacher.		
e	Sylvia is a lawyer.		

Grammar

Describing places and people

You met adjectives (describing words) briefly in the first unit. Now let's have a look at them in more detail. Generally speaking, adjectives in Portuguese, unlike in English, go after the thing or person they are describing, e.g. **uma empresa internacional** *an international company*. This does not apply if you are talking about something introduced by the verb *to be* e.g. **Londres é grande** *London is big*, where the word order is the same as in English.

The important point to remember is that if you are describing something (or someone) that is feminine, or in the plural, you must make the adjective match it by changing its ending – this is known as 'agreement of the adjective and noun'. Many adjectives end in -o (the masculine standard), such as **movimentado**. Look how it changes: **movimentado, movimentada, movimentados, movimentadas**. A busy city is **uma cidade movimentada** (fem), and two busy countries are **dois países movimentados** (masculine, plural).

Be on the look-out for irregular-ending words. In the dialogue you had **grande, interessante** and **internacional**:

m	f	mpl	fpl
grande	grande	grandes	grandes
interessante	interessante	interessantes	interessantes
internacional	internacional	internacionais	internacionais

Here are some adjectives you may want to use to describe your town (*town/city* = **a cidade** = fem.).

You will meet more adjectives as you progress.

pequeno *small*
barulhento *noisy*
histórico *historic(al)*
sossegado *quiet*
cultural *cultural*

lindo/bonito *pretty*
industrial *industrial*
litoral *coastal*
sujo *dirty*
agricultural *agricultural*

Ter *To have*

You have now met various parts of the verb **ter** *to have*. Here it is in full for you to learn:

(eu) tenho	*I have*	**(nós) temos**	*we have*
(tu) tens*	*you have*		
(ele/ela) tem	*he/she/it has*	**(eles/elas) têm**	*they have*
(você) tem	*you have*	**(vocês) têm**	*you have* (plural)

*As this form is used in only some parts of Brazil, henceforth we shall concentrate on just four verbal forms. You will hear some Brazilians use **tu** plus the verb for **você**. Whilst being grammatically incorrect, it is nevertheless a colloquially recognized usage in some areas.

Note that **Ter** is used when you talk about your age, and not the verb *To be*, e.g. *I am 15* = **Tenho 15 anos.**

What is/are your/their name/s?

There are different ways to express names in Portuguese. You can say:

Qual é (seu) nome? *What is (your) name?* Or **Como (você) se chama?** *What are (you) called?* Or even **Quem é (você)?** *Who are (you)/Who is…?*

Answers may be: **(meu) nome é …** *(my) name is …* Or **me chamo/ se chama …** *(I) am/…..is called …* Or **sou/é …** *I am/s/he is …*

In the dialogue you were introduced to:

Como eles se chamam? *What are they called?*, and **Qual é o nome dele?** *What is his name?* Both of these are dealt with in following sections.

Verbs – present tense

In Portuguese, the ending of the verb (the action word) changes according to whoever is carrying out the action (the verb's subject). It is vital to get straight at this point the fact that it does not matter if the person is male or female, but whether they are 1st person (*I, we*), 2nd (*you*) or 3rd (*he, she, it, they*). Many people become confused when first approaching these verb forms, as they have just managed to master the concept of the **o/a** endings for male and female nouns and adjectives. Although these endings also appear on some verbs, they are NOT related to gender. In Portuguese there are three main groups of verbs, as well as a variety of irregular oddities. The main groups are: Group 1 ending in **ar** – the most common; Group 2 ending in **er**; Group 3 ending in **ir**. The last two are very similar in endings. With only a few exceptions, all these verbs are formed in the same way:

Let's take a verb that you met in the dialogue and see what changes happen to it when we want different people to carry out the action.

You had examples of the verb to work (**trabalhar**): **trabalho** – *I work* and **trabalha** – *he works/you work*.

▶ First you take off the (**-ar**) ending and you are left with what is called the stem, e.g. **trabalhar** (*to work*) – **trabalh**.
▶ Then you add on to this stem the appropriate ending according to whoever is doing the action.
▶ For **-ar** verbs, the endings you require are as follows:

stem +		
-o	*I*	**trabalho**
-a	*he, she, it, you*	**trabalha**
-amos	*we*	**trabalhamos**
-am	*they, you* (plural)	**trabalham**

Here are a few examples:

falo	*I speak*	**gostamos**	*we like*
trabalha	*he/she/it works/you work*	**moram**	*they, you live*

The meanings are sometimes ambiguous, so to make sure you really know who is doing the action, you may need to use the words for *he* (**ele**), *she* (**ela**), or *they* (**eles, elas**).

More verbs!

Some verbs are not content with changing their endings, but also have a little word accompanying them: **Se**. This word here means *self* or *selves*, so the question **Como eles se chamam?** actually means *what do they call themselves?* These 'self' words are known as 'reflexive pronouns', and they make the verb into a reflexive verb.

The full set you need to know is:

me	*myself*	**nos**	*ourselves*
se	*his/her/yourself/itself*	**se**	*them/yourselves*

You will see that they are placed before the verb. If you were
in Portugal or speaking with a Portuguese person, they would
usually place them afterwards. If you learnt some Portuguese
before starting this course you may discover that in Brazil many
of the rules of grammar are much more flexible than
in Portugal.

More possessives: 'his/her'

To say *his/her* (and the plural *their*), in Portuguese, you should
say *the (thing) of him/her/them*, as in the dialogue: **Qual é o nome
dele?** *What is the name of him? (What is his name?)*

The full forms are:

o/a ... dele	*his*	**o/a ... dela**	*her*
os/as ... dele	*his* (pl.)	**os/as ... dela**	*her* (pl.)
o/a ... deles	*their* (m)	**o/a ... delas**	*their* (f)
os/as ... deles	*their*	**os/as ... delas**	*their*
e.g as chaves deles	*their keys*	**o nome dela**	*her name*

You will also hear **seu/s (sua/s)**, the same form as *your*, but as this
can cause confusion, it's better to use the other forms unless the
context is completely unambiguous.

Compare **seu nome** *his/her/its/your name* and **o nome dele** *his/its*
name.

Numa *In a*

Numa is actually two words squashed together (or contracted)
for ease of pronunciation. They are: **em** (*in/on*) + **uma** (*a, fem.*) –
Numa (*in/on a*), e.g. **numa escola** = *in a school*.

You will also find **num (em + um)**, **nuns (em + uns)** and **numas (em + umas)**, e.g. **nuns apartamentos** *in some rooms*.

In written Portuguese the two words often appear separated (e.g. **em uma …**) although in practice people run them together when speaking.

Ser + *professions*

To talk about your, or other people's professions, you use **ser** (*to be*) plus the name of the profession, e.g. **sou professora** *I am a teacher*.

Note that there is no equivalent here to the English word *a*.

Here is a check list of some professions you may need to use. If yours is not here, your dictionary or teacher should be able to help you.

professor/a *teacher*	**médico/a** *doctor*
engenheiro/a *engineer*	**advogado/a** *lawyer*
o/a dentista *dentist*	**recepcionista** *receptionist*
o/a motorista *driver*	**o/a gerente** *manager*
o/a estudante *student*	**secretário/a** *secretary*

The full set of forms for **ser** is:

eu sou	*I am*	**nós somos**	*we are*
ele/ela é	*s/he, it is*	**eles/elas são**	*they are*
você é	*you are*	**vocês são**	*you (pl.) are*

Languages, nationalities

So far you have met **inglesa** (*English woman*) and **português** (*Portuguese*). Words of nationality, used also to describe the place of origin of something, are adjectives, and the name of any language is the masculine singular form. Look at the following table for more examples. Portuguese does not use capital letters for words of nationality.

	Nationality masc. sing.	fem. sing.	masc. pl.	fem. pl.	Language spoken
Brazilian	brasileiro	brasileira	brasileiros	brasileiras	português
Portuguese	português	portuguesa	portugueses	portuguesas	português
English	inglês	inglesa	ingleses	inglesas	inglês
American	americano	americana	americanos	americanas	inglês
Spanish	espanhol	espanhola	espanhois	espanholas	espanhol
Argentine	argentino	argentina	argentinos	argentinas	espanhol
Chilean	chileno	chilena	chilenos	chilenas	espanhol
French	francês	francesa	franceses	francesas	francês
German	alemão	alemã	alemães	alemãs	alemão
Greek	grego	grega	gregos	gregas	grego

Dialogue 2

José wants to note down some of Sylvia's details so that they can maintain links in the future.

José	Qual é seu endereço em Manchester Sylvia?
Sylvia	Oitenta e cinco Manor, m-a-n-o-r Road, Manchester, Inglaterra.
José	Tem telefone?
Sylvia	Sim, o número é 0161–236–553218, e o número do fax é 0161–236–553222.
José	Está bem. E tem telefone aqui no hotel?
Sylvia	Sim, estou no hotel Felix, o número é 678990, e estou no apartamento 15.

QV

endereço (o) *address*
oitenta e cinco *eighty-five*
Inglaterra *England*

telefone (o) *telephone*
no hotel *in the hotel*
estou *I am*

True or false?

Say if these statements are **verdadeiro** or **falso**.

		V	F
a	Sylvia lives at 83 Manor Rd.		
b	She has no phone.		
c	She is in the Felix Hotel.		

Grammar

More numbers

◀) **CD1, TR 3, 03:07**

Unfortunately, you cannot escape numbers – they surround us in everyday situations – money, time, dates. Here is another set for you to start learning.

21	vinte e um/uma	**50**	cinquenta
22	vinte e dois/duas	**60**	sessenta
23	vinte e três	**70**	setenta
24	vinte e quatro	**80**	oitenta
25	vinte e cinco	**90**	noventa
30	trinta	**100**	cem (cento)
31	trinta e um/uma	**101**	cento e um
40	quarenta		

The word **e** (*and*) is used to join the two lots of digits together.

46 – **quarenta e seis**   89 – **oitenta e nove**

Cem is used for a round *100* and **cento** for *101* and beyond.

Estar *To be*

To say where you are temporarily, you must use **estar**, the verb *to be* that describes anything temporary, including location e.g. **Estou no hotel** *I am in the hotel.*

The full set of forms for this verb are:

eu estou	*I am*	**nós estamos**	*we are*
ele/ela está	*he/she/it is*	**eles/elas estão**	*they are*
você está	*you are*	**vocês estão**	*you* (pl.) *are*

No hotel *In the hotel*

No is another example of a contracted pair of words, in this case **em + o** (*the*). It means *in the* or *on the*. You will also find **na = em + a, nos = em + os, nas = em + as** (**nas cidades** *in the towns*).

You will also discover that the word **de** (*of, from*) contracts in the same way: **do/da/dos/das** e.g. **A chave do hotel** *the key of the hotel* (the hotel's key).

Countries

Most countries in Portuguese also fall into either a masculine or feminine group. Here are some examples:

Masculine countries		**Feminine countries**	
o Brasil	*Brazil*	**a Inglaterra**	*England*
o Canadá	*Canada*	**a França**	*France*
o México	*Mexico*	**a Alemanha**	*Germany*
o Japão	*Japan*	**a Argentina**	*Argentina*
o Peru	*Peru*	**a Itália**	*Italy*
o Reino Unido	*the UK*	**a China**	*China*
os Estados Unidos	*the USA*	**a Espanha**	*Spain*

So, to say *I am from England* you should say: **sou da (de + a) Inglaterra**, using the contracted form of **da**. Not everyone follows this rule, though, so you will also hear '**sou de Inglaterra**' etc.

Insight

When out at a café, Brazilians love to drink their **cafezinho** *little coffee* (strong, dark espresso), or when it's hot the **chope** – *cooled draught national lager*, the most well known being **Antártica**. One of this company's ads for its lager used to have the slogan **estupidamente gelada** *stupidly chilled* – it certainly makes sense when the temperature rises!

Insight

When giving someone a telephone number, if there is a six in the number, the Brazilians often say **meia** (*half*), and not **seis**.

Test yourself

como é...?	*what's ... like?*
como se chama/m ...?	*what is/are he/she/you/they called?*
qual é o (seu) nome?	*what's (your) name?*
tem ... anos	*is ... years old*
qual é seu endereço?	*what's your address?*
o número do telefone/fax é...	*the telephone/fax number is ...*
Londres é barulhento	*London is noisy*
Trabalho num hotel	*I work in a hotel*
Sou medico	*I am a doctor*
Somos americanas	*We are Americans*

Practice

Complete your part of the dialogue. José is trying to find out more about you.

José	Você é de Liverpool?
You	*(Say no, I'm from Birmingham.)*
José	Como é a cidade de Birmingham?
	(Contd)

You	*(Say it's big and industrial.)*
José	Tem filhos?
You	*(Say yes, I have one son.)*
José	Qual é o nome dele?
You	*(Say he is called David. He is 28 years old and is a French teacher.)*
José	Você trabalha?
You	*(Say yes, I work for an international company.)*

2 Match up the telephone numbers in digits and Portuguese.

   a quatro dois um cinco três três   **i** 368475
   b seis seis oito quatro quatro zero   **ii** 553311
   c três meia oito quatro sete cinco   **iii** 421533
   d cinco cinco três três um um   **iv** 904621
   e nove zero quatro meia dois um   **v** 668440

◄» **CD1, TR 3, 03:45**

3 Listen to someone describing their family, work and town, and tick which pictures apply to the descriptions given.

1 a

4 Fill in the gaps with appropriate words for numbers/nouns/adjectives.

   a Tenho (5) _____ chaves (small) _____.

   b Sra Ferreira é _____ (Brazilian).

   c Sylvia tem três _____ _____ (interesting, children).

   d Sou de Paris; é uma cidade _____ (historic).

   e Marli tem _____ _____ _____ (2, German wines).

Testing yourself – do you understand?

One of Marli's students has received a letter from a new penfriend. Can you read it and answer the questions on it?

Brasília, 8 de janeiro

Oi Maria,

Tudo bem? Eu estou muito bem. Vou te dizer um pouco sobre quem sou. Meu nome é Vânia, tenho vinte e dois anos e sou de Brasília.

É uma cidade super-grande e moderna, e muito interessante. Não sou casada. Sou estudante de línguas e também trabalho numa escola secundária; sou secretária.

Tchau, Vânia

vou te dizer um pouco sobre quem sou *I'm going to tell you a bit about who I am*

1 How old is Vânia?
2 What is Brasília like?
3 Is she married?
4 What does she do?
5 Now write a short letter like this about yourself.

(You will find an example in the Key to the exercises.)

3

Onde é sua cidade?
Where is your town?

In this unit you will learn
- *How to describe where your home town is*
- *How to describe your belongings and recover lost property*
- *How to describe what things are made of*
- *About colours*

Dialogue 1

Sylvia goes to the Ferreiras' house to arrange her stay there. She chats to the daily help (**a faxineira**), Dona Rita.

● CD1, TR 4, 00:10

Sylvia	Bom dia. Sou Sylvia Peters, amiga da senhora Ferreira.
D. Rita	Bom dia, senhora. Como está?
Sylvia	Bem, obrigada, e a senhora?
D. Rita	Eu estou bem, graças a Deus.
Sylvia	Marli está?
D. Rita	Ela já vem da escola. A senhora não é daqui, é?
Sylvia	Não, sou inglesa. Sou de Manchester.
D. Rita	E como é a sua cidade? É uma cidade grande como aqui? Onde é? Perto de Londres?
Sylvia	Bom, Manchester é uma cidade interessante e bastante grande, mas não como São Paulo.

(Contd)

D. Rita	E sua família mora lá com você?
Sylvia	Mora, sim, mas também tenho família no centro da Inglaterra, em Birmingham, e também numa cidade pequena ao sul do país, perto de Londres. Manchester não é perto de Londres, mas ao noroeste do país.
D. Rita	Aqui está a senhora Ferreira. Vão pegar suas malas, não é?
Sylvia	Sim, vamos para o hotel agora e voltamos para o jantar.

amiga (a) *friend*
estou bem *I'm well*
graças a Deus *thank goodness*
Marli está? *is Marli at home?*
ela já vem *she's on her way*
daqui *from here*
como aqui *like here*
bastante grande *quite big*
não como ... *not like ...*
mora *live*
lá *there*
onde é *where is?*

com *with*
no centro de *in the centre of*
ao sul de *to the south of*
país (o) *country*
perto de *near to*
ao noroeste de *in the northwest of*
pegar *to get/fetch*
malas (as) *suitcases*
vamos *we're going*
agora *now*
voltamos *we'll return*
jantar (o) *dinner*

True or false?

Tick **verdadeiro** or **falso** for the following statements based on the dialogue.

V   F

a Marli está em casa (at home).
b Sylvia tem família em Manchester.
c Londres é longe de Manchester.
d Marli e Sylvia vão para o hotel.
e Elas vão jantar no hotel.

Grammar

X's friend

When talking about possession in the 3rd person (he/she/it/they), remember you learnt to say *the (thing) of him/her*, etc. in Unit 2. The same applies if you want to use alternatives to him/her, such as *the teacher's key*, *the student's room*, etc. You must turn the sentence around in Portuguese and say:

the key of the teacher – **a chave do professor** (da professora)
the room of the students – **o apartamento dos estudantes**

In the dialogue you met '**amiga da senhora Ferreira**' – *Mrs Ferreira's friend*.

> ## Insight
> 'Mr' and 'Mrs'
>
> The expressions for *Mr* and *Mrs* are **(o) senhor (sr)** and **(a) senhora (sra)**. These combine with words such as **de** to form **do sr/da sra**, e.g. **a casa do senhor Villas Boas** *Mr Villas Boas' house*.

Locations

If you are describing where your home town or place of work is, the following may be useful:

no/*ao norte (de) *in/to the north (of)*   **no/ao leste** *in the east*
no/ao sul *in the south*   **no/ao oeste** *in the west*
ao/no centro (de) *in the centre (of)*   **na costa** *on the coast*
no interior *inland*   **no litoral** *on the coast*
perto de *near*   **longe de** *far (from)*

*ao = a (*to/at*) + o (*the*). Other contractions involving the word a (which is known as a preposition – a locating word) are:

a + a = à   vamos à cidade *we're going to the town/city*
a + os = aos vamos aos hotéis *we're going to the hotels*
a + as = às   vamos às lojas *we're going to the shops*

Try not to be thrown off balance by the fact that the word a in Portuguese also means *the* in the feminine form.

Liverpool é ao norte da Inglaterra.	*Liverpool is in the north of England.*
Brasília é no centro do Brasil.	*Brasília is in the centre of Brazil.*
Campinas é no interior de São Paulo.	*Campinas is in the interior of São Paulo (State).*

Ir *To go*

You met parts of this important irregular verb in the dialogue: **vão** – *you* (pl.) *are going*, and **vamos** – *we're going* (also meaning *let's …*).

In full, the verb is:

vou	*I'm going/I go*	**vamos**	*we're going/go*
vai	*s/he's going/s/he goes*	**vão**	*they're going/they go*
	you're going/you go		*you're going/you go* (pl.)
	it's going/it goes		

You can use it to say what you do on a regular basis (**vou à escola** – *I go to school*), or what you are going to do (**vamos ao centro** – *we're going to the town centre*). **Vamos** also means *'let's go'*.

Dialogue 2

Sylvia realizes she left her bag in the taxi on the way to the Ferreiras'. Marli takes her to the taxi lost property office (**a seção de perdidos e achados**) where she talks to an employee (**empregado**).

Empregado	Bom, vamos ver. Uma bolsa, sim?
Sylvia	Isso. É bem pequena.
Empregado	E de que é? De couro, de plástico, de quê?
Sylvia	De couro.
Empregado	E de que cor é?
Sylvia	Preta e roxa.
Empregado	E tem alguma coisa dentro?
Sylvia	Sim, tem a chave do hotel, uma carteira com dinheiro, minha agenda, e meus óculos de sol amarelos.
Empregado	É esta? *(shows her a bag)*
Sylvia	Sim, é. Obrigada. É muito gentil.
Empregado	De nada. Faça o favor de assinar aqui. Bom dia.

bolsa (a) *bag*
carteira (a) *purse/wallet*
de que é *what's it (made) of?*
dinheiro (o) *money*
agenda (a) *diary*
é bem pequena *it's really small*
(de) couro *leather*
óculos de sol (os) *sunglasses*
(de) plástico *plastic*
de que cor é? *what colour is it?*
amarelos *yellow*
preto *black*
gentil *kind*
roxo *purple*
faça o favor de assinar *please sign*
alguma coisa *something*
dentro *inside*

Exercise

Answer **sim** *yes* or **não** *no* to these statements.

a A bolsa de Sylvia é de couro. _____
b É preta. _____
c Tem o passaporte dentro. _____

Grammar

De que é (feito)? *What's it (made) of?*

To describe what something is made from, Portuguese often uses
the structure: a (thing) of (material). Look at these examples:

De:	plástico	*plastic*	papel	*paper*
	couro	*leather*	lã	*wool*
	vidro	*glass*	algodão	*cotton*
	metal	*metal*	pedra	*stone*
	madeira	*wood*	tijolo	*brick/tile*

e.g. **uma bolsa de plástico** *a plastic bag*, **uma toalha de algodão**
a cotton towel. You can of course find examples such as **uma bolsa
plástica** and **uma chave metálica**, where adjectives are used rather
than the name of the material itself.

Colours

You will also need to know **as cores** *colours* to describe personal
possessions, or even features of people (eyes, etc.).

Remember that **as cores** *colours* are adjectives. They must change
their endings where appropriate to match the noun(s) they are
describing. They also go after the noun, e.g.

QUICK VOCAB

preto *black*
branco *white*
roxo *purple*
azul
(pl. = azuis) *blue*
amarelo *yellow*
escuro *dark*

verde *green*
marrom
(pl. = marrons) *brown*
vermelho *red*
(cor de) laranja *orange*
(cor de) rosa *pink*
claro *light*

uma chave branca	a white key
dois passaportes azuis	two blue passports
óculos marrons escuros	dark brown glasses
um carro laranja	an orange car

Insight
'Please'

One of the polite ways of asking people to do things is by using the structure of **faça o favor de** + verb. This is literally *do the favour of … ing*. You can use it with any verb. To ask more than one person to do something, change **faça** to **façam**. For example, **Façam o favor de trabalhar** *Please work*.

Ser/Estar – an overview

You learnt the formation for these two verbs in the last unit. Let's look more closely at when you should use each one.

ser

Professions	**Sou professora**
Nationality	**É inglesa?**
Permanent location	**É no centro**
Permanent characteristics	**É grande/preto**
Place of origin	**Sou de …**

estar

Temporary location	**Aqui está**
Temporary condition	**Como está?**
Position	**Está dentro**

Bags and briefcases

Here are some suggestions for vocabulary you may need when describing the contents of your bag.

o passaporte *passport*
o celular (o telemóvel) *mobile phone*
uma caneta *pen*
um lenço *handkerchief*
os comprimidos *tablets*
o livro de endereços *address book*
os bilhetes de ... *tickets for ...*
um pente *comb*
o batom *lipstick*
o isqueiro *cigarette lighter*
as chaves *keys*

Test yourself

como é sua cidade?	*what's your town like?*
onde é (sua cidade?)	*where is it (your town)?*
... é uma cidade ...	*... is a ... town*
é grande/interessante/pequena	*it's big/interesting/small*
ao norte/sul/leste/oeste	*to/in the north/south/east/west*
faça/m o favor de ...	*please ...*
de que é feito?	*what's it made of?*
é de couro/vidro/lã	*it's made of leather/glass/wool*
de que cor é?	*what colour is it?*
é preto/azul/vermelho	*it's black/blue/red*

Practice

1 Decide which verb *to be* (**ser/estar**) you should use in each example, and write the correct form of it.

   a José _____ do Brasil.
   b As cidades _____ grandes.
   c Minha chave _____ dentro da bolsa.
   d João tem um filho; ele _____ médico.
   e _____ Ángela, _____ americana.

2 Fill in your part of the dialogue, about where you're from.

Sônia	Você é de Nova Iorque, não é?
You	*(Say no, I'm from Brighton.)*
Sônia	Onde é Brighton?
You	*(Say it's a small town in the south of England.)*
Sônia	É perto de Londres?
You	*(Say yes, it's quite near.)*

CD1, TR 4, 03:05

3 Listen to someone describing their bag and its contents. Tick the relevant pictures below, according to what you hear.

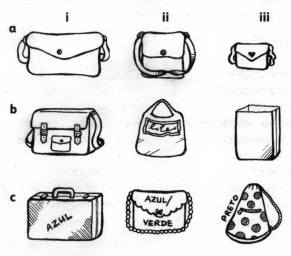

4 Look at the map below and listen to the description of where certain towns are located. See if you can correctly mark where the towns should be.

São Paulo state

São Paulo capital

1 =
2 =
3 =
4 =
5 =

Choose from:

Santos	Uberaba
Piracicaba	
Campinas	Catanduva

Testing yourself – do you understand?

Look at the following postcard, and say if the statements below are **verdadeiro** or **falso**.

> oi Paulo,
>
> Estou num hotel no centro da Inglaterra. A cidade é pequena, mas é perto de Birmingham que é grande e interessante.
>
> Um beijo da
> Ana
>
> Paulo R. da Silva
> R. Mem Martin, 25
> Piracicaba-SP
> 10325
> Brasil

	V	**F**

1 Ana is staying with relatives.
2 She is in the Northwest of England.
3 The town is not far from Birmingham.
4 She thinks Birmingham is boring.

Há uma farmácia por aqui?

Is there a chemist's around here?

In this unit you will learn
- *How to ask for and understand basic directions*
- *How to talk about the weather*
- *How to understand time*
- *How to say there is/there are*

Dialogue 1

Sylvia pops into the city centre (**o centro**). First of all she needs a chemist.

CD1, TR 5, 00:10

Sylvia	Desculpe. Há uma farmácia por aqui?
Transeunte	*(passer-by)* Aqui, nesta rua não há, mas há uma na Rua Cabral.
Sylvia	E onde é esta rua?
Transeunte	Bem, você vai por aqui em frente, vira à esquerda naquela esquina, depois você segue em frente mais um pouco, toma a segunda à direita, e a farmácia é aí.
Sylvia	Fica muito longe?
Transeunte	Não, é só dez minutos.
Sylvia	Obrigada.

desculpe *excuse me*
há *there is/are; is/are there?*
farmácia (a) *chemist's*
por aqui *round here*
nesta rua não há *there isn't one in this street* ❓
mas *but*
você: vai/vira/segue/toma *you: go/turn/follow/take*
em frente *in front/ahead*
à esquerda/direita *on the left/right*
mais um pouco *a little more*
a segunda *the second*
é aí *it's there*
fica muito longe? *is it a long way off?*
é só dez minutos *it's only ten minutes*
naquela esquina *on that street corner*

Exercise 1

Can you answer the following questions based on the dialogue?

	Yes	No
a Is there a chemist's where Sylvia is?		
b Does Sylvia have to turn left?		
c Is the chemist's a long way off?		

Grammar

Is there ...?

To ask if there is a particular shop near where you are, you say **há** (*is/are there*) [*a shop*] **por aqui?** You can also talk about such locations as: **aqui perto/perto daqui** – *near (to) here*, **nesta rua/cidade** – *in this street/town*. If you are lucky, the answer will be: **sim, há.** In the dialogue the answer was negative (**não há**), but at least the passer-by helpfully explained where the nearest chemist's was.

You can also use **tem...?** as an alternative to **há. Tem um banco perto daqui?** *Is there a bank near here?*

To be more specific in your request for information, use: **onde é?** – *where is?* or **onde há/tem** – *where is there (a)?* Understanding the directions is another matter!

Directions

To begin with you need to know your basic directions:

à esquerda <	**em frente ^**	**à direita >**
(to/on the) left	*straight on*	*(to/on the) right*

Then, some basic instructions:

você vai	*you go*
vira	*turn*
segue	*carry on*
toma	*take*

And you will finally discover what you're looking for:

e ... é aí/fica aí/é por aí – *and ... is over there*

You may want to check: **fica longe/perto?** – *is it a long way/near?* or **é longe daqui?** – *is it a long way from here?* If you're lucky the answer will be: **é perto!**

You may well make use of expressions such as:

Pode repetir por favor? *Can you repeat that please?*
Não compreendo muito bem. *I don't understand very well.*
Fale mais devagar. *Speak more slowly.*

Nesta, naquela *In this, in that*

These are two more examples of contracted words. **Nesta** comes from **em + esta** (*this*) (you met the other forms of **esta** in Unit 1).

Naquela comes from **em + aquela** (*that*). The full forms of *that/those* are:

aquele (m.)	**aquela (f.)**	**aqueles (m. pl.)**	**aquelas (f. pl.)**

aquele senhor	*that man*	**aquelas ruas**	*those streets*
naquela rua	*in that street*	**naqueles livros**	*in those books*

First to fifth

◀) **CD1, TR 5, 01:05**

When requesting directions, you also need to know some ordinal numbers (i.e. the numbers used for putting things in numerical order), so that you can turn down the appropriate street. Here are a few to get you going. You will need more of them if you are visiting people who live on the 20th floors of high-rise blocks!

1st	**primeiro**	*2nd*	**segundo**	*3rd*	**terceiro**
4th	**quarto**	*5th*	**quinto**		

These are adjectives and as such will change their endings to agree with the noun they are describing, e.g. *the second key* = **a segunda chave**, *the 4th street* = **a quarta rua**. They are placed before the noun, unlike most other adjectives.

Dialogue 2

Sylvia now needs to find a bank.

Sylvia	Desculpe. Sabe se há um banco perto daqui?
Transeunte	Sim, há um banco no fim da rua, à direita.
Sylvia	E sabe se está aberto agora?
Transeunte	Que horas são?
Sylvia	São onze e meia.
Transeunte	Então, sim, está aberto. Aqui os bancos abrem das oito e meia da manhã até às três horas da tarde.

◀ CD1, TR 5, 01:20

QUICK VOCAB

sabe se *do you know if/whether*
no fim da rua *at the end of the street*
está aberto *is open*
que horas são? *what time is it?*
são onze e meia *it's 11.30*
então *well then*
os bancos abrem *the banks open*
das 8 e meia da manhã *from 8.30 in the morning*
até às 3 horas da tarde *until 3 pm*

True or false?

Say whether the following are **verdadeiro** (V) or **falso** (F).

a Há um banco perto.
b O banco não está aberto.
c Os bancos abrem até às 4 horas da tarde.

_____

Grammar

Spend, spend, spend!!!

Here is a check-list of some of the shops and establishments you
may need to talk about.

QUICK VOCAB

as lojas *shops*	**o correio** *post office*
o mercado *market*	**a farmácia** *chemist's*
o supermercado *supermarket*	**o turismo** *tourist information*
o hotel *hotel*	
o restaurante *restaurant*	**a loja de roupas** *clothes shop*
o café *café*	
o banco *bank*	**o açougue** *butcher's*
a padaria *baker's*	**a peixaria** *fishmonger's*
a sapataria *shoe shop*	**a drogaria** *drugstore*
a mercearia *grocer's*	**a livraria** *book store*

You will find more on shops in Unit 7.

Time

To ask the time you say **Que horas são?** – literally *what hours are they?* Answers will be:

São duas horas. São três horas. São quatro horas. São cinco horas.

São seis horas. São sete horas. São oito horas. São nove horas.

São dez horas. São onze horas. São doze horas.

É meio-dia/meia-noite/uma hora – *It's midday/midnight/one o'clock*

Time past the hour is expressed as:

X (horas) e Y (minutos), e.g. **São cinco e vinte** *It's twenty past five. Quarter and half past* are: **X e um quarto/X e meia** or **X e quinze/X e trinta**.

Time to the hour is expressed as minutes to (**para**) the next hour, e.g. **São dez para as oito** = *it's ten to eight.*

Opening and closing times: **aberto/a** = *open* and **fechado/a** = *closed.*

People will express shop times as follows: … **abre/fecha** (**está aberto/fechado**) **das** … (**horas**) **até às** … **horas**. *It opens/closes (it's open/closed) from …. (o'clock) until …. o'clock.* e.g. **O turismo abre das nove e um quarto até às dez para as cinco** = *The tourist office opens from 9.15 till 4.50.*

This can be qualified with the part of the day in question: **da manhã/da tarde/da noite** – *in the morning/in the afternoon/at night*, e.g. **até às três horas da tarde** = *until three in the afternoon.*

Dialogue 3

Sylvia stops at the **quiosque** in the square to buy a newspaper (**um jornal**).

Sylvia	Boa tarde. Uma 'Folha de São Paulo' por favor.
Vendedora *(vendor)*	São 2 reais.
Sylvia	Que calor, não é?
Vendedora	Pois é, hoje está muito quente. A senhora não é daqui, é?
Sylvia	Não, sou inglesa.
Vendedora	Ah, na Inglaterra sempre chove, não é?
Sylvia	Chove muito, mas no verão também faz calor. Mas aqui na cidade não venta, e está muito abafado.
Vendedora	É sempre assim – ainda pior por causa da poluição aqui. Eu não aguento estes dias.
Sylvia	Nem eu. Bom, tenho de ir. Tchau.

QUICK VOCAB

Folha de São Paulo *São Paulo daily paper*
por favor *please*
que calor *isn't it hot (lit. what heat)*
são … reais *that's … reais*
hoje *today*
quente *hot*
sempre *always*

chove it rains
no verão in the summer
faz calor it's hot
abafado stifling/close
é sempre assim it's always like this
ainda pior even worse
por causa de because of
poluição (a) pollution
não aguento I can't stand
nem eu me neither
tenho de ir I have to go

Exercise 2

See if you have understood the dialogue. Choose the correct answers from the boxes.

1 How much is the paper? **a** 2 reais **b** 3 reais

2 The vendor thinks in England it's always **a** raining **b** windy

3 One of the contributing factors to the heavy atmosphere is **a** pollution **b** clouds

Grammar

The weather

There are various ways to describe **o tempo** *the weather*:

Verb		Expressions			
fazer	to do/make	**faz calor**	it's hot	**faz frio**	it's cold
estar	to be	**está quente**	it's hot	**está frio**	it's cold
		está abafado	it's close		
chover	to rain			**chove**	it rains
nevar	to snow			**neva**	it snows

Ser is only used with weather expressions if you are describing a permanent state, such as climate: **É sempre frio no inverno no Canadá** – *It's always cold in winter in Canada*.

Insight

Most shops in Brazil open from 8.30 to 6.30. On Saturdays they open until lunchtime, and it is rare to find anything except cafés or large shopping centres open on Sundays.

Insight

The summer months can become quite intolerable heat-wise, especially if you are away from the coast. Remember the seasons in Brazil are the opposite to the northern hemisphere. The hottest time is January–March.

Insight

Brazilian currency is the **real** (pl. **reais**). Inflation in Brazil is notorious for its eccentricity, running over 100% and more, although in recent years it has shown signs of steadying.

Insight

Some Brazilian publications are available outside the country and make good reading practice. You could try getting hold of *Folha de São Paulo*, or *Veja* (like *Time*).

Test yourself

há/tem um/a … por aqui?	*is there a … round here?*
à esquerda/direita	*on the left/right*
fica (muito) longe/perto?	*is it (very) far/near?*
a segunda rua …	*the second street …*
está aberto/fechado?	*is it open/closed?*
são … horas	*it's … o'clock*

abrem das … até às …	*they open from … to …*
da manhã/tarde/noite	*in the morning/afternoon/evening*
por favor	*please*
está quente/frio	*it's hot/cold*

Practice

1 Can you do the following?
   a ask if there is a butcher's near here
   b ask where there is a post office
   c ask what time it is
   d say it's 2.30 pm
   e say in Germany it rains a little

2 Look at the clocks below and match them to the times given.

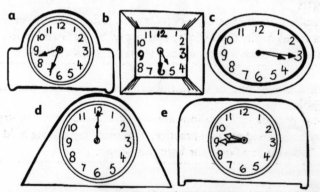

i são cinco e meia **ii** é meio-dia/meia noite **iii** são vinte e cinco
para as nove **iv** são três e um quarto **v** é um quarto para as dez

3 Look at the map overleaf, then read the directions. In each
   case say where you would end up if you correctly followed the
   instructions.
   Instructions: starting outside your hotel (*on map).
   a Vira à esquerda, toma a segunda rua à direita, e vai em
   frente. _____ fica na esquina.

b Vai em frente, e _____ é ali à direita. É muito perto.

c Vira à esquerda, segue em frente um pouco, depois toma a primeira à esquerda, e _____ é ali em frente.

d Vai em frente, e segue a rua um pouco. Toma a segunda à esquerda, depois vira à esquerda, e toma a primeira à direita. _____ é aí em frente.

◄)) CD1, TR 5, 02:52

4 Listen to someone describing the weather today in various countries (England, Brazil, France, Mexico, Japan) and link up the weather pictures with the appropriate country.

5 Fill in your part of this dialogue. You are trying to find out about the local market.

You	*(Say excuse me. Do you know if there is a market near here?)*
Transeunte	Sim, há um no fim da rua.
You	*(Say do you know if it is open now.)*
Transeunte	Que horas são?
You	*(Say it's 10.15.)*
Transeunte	Então, sim, está aberto.
You	*(Ask is it far?)*
Transeunte	Não, é só cinco minutos.
You	*(Say thanks and goodbye.)*

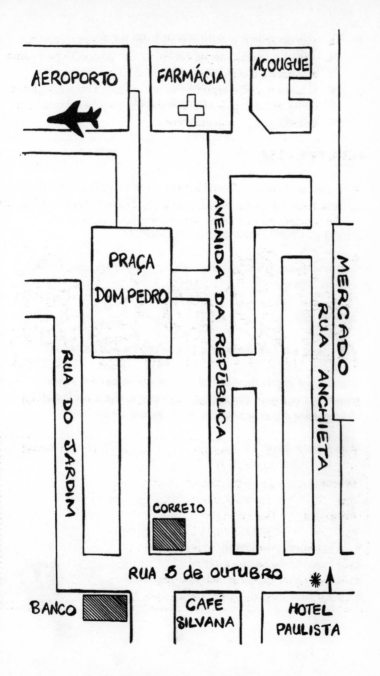

6 Fill in the gaps below with words from the box.

    a Onde _____ o mercado?

    b É _____ em frente.

    c _____ são meus filhos.

    d Toma a _____ rua à esquerda.

    e São dez _____ as oito.

---

aqueles	terceira	fica	para	ali

Testing yourself – do you understand?

Read this message that has been left for Sylvia, and answer the questions below.

Sylvia

Pode fazer um favor para mim, e ir ao correio com as cartas?

Vai daqui à esquerda, vira à direita na rua Gomes Sá, e toma a segunda à esquerda que é a rua Nascimento. O correio fica ali em frente. Abre das nove e quinze até às quatro da tarde.

Não é muito longe!

Obrigada

Marli.

1 Where does Marli want Sylvia to go?

2 Where should she turn right?

3 Which street on the left should she take?

4 What time does the place close?

5 Is it very far?

5

A que horas começa?
What time do you start?

In this unit you will learn
- *How to discuss your work*
- *How to discuss how you travel to work*
- *How to talk about daily routines*

Dialogue 1

Sylvia and the Ferreiras have gone on a trip to Santos, the most important port on the southern Brazilian coast.

Sylvia	Meu Deus! É tão grande – e movimentado. Quantas pessoas trabalham aqui?	◆ CD1, TR 6, 00:10
José	Não sei exatamente, mas deve ser um número enorme. É o porto mais importante do Brasil.	
Marli	É mais importante do que Liverpool. Você vê todos os barcos ali? Vêm de toda parte do mundo.	
Sylvia	Incrível. Marli, me diga uma coisa – a escola onde você trabalha – tem quantos alunos?	
Marli	Tem mais ou menos cento e vinte alunos – dos catorze aos vinte e cinco anos.	
Sylvia	Então, é uma escola bastante grande. Você come lá durante o dia?	

(Contd)

Marli	Não, a escola não tem refeitório mas eu almoço num café bem perto.
Sylvia	A que horas começa?
Marli	Começo às oito e um quarto, tenho uma hora e meia para o almoço, e saio às seis da tarde. Às vezes tenho uma turma à noite.
Sylvia	Tanto trabalho!
Marli	É mesmo!

QUICK VOCAB

meu Deus! *my God/goodness me*
tão *so*
quantas pessoas *how many people*
não sei exatamente *I don't know exactly*
deve ser *it must be*
enorme *enormous*
porto (o) *port*
o mais importante do Brasil *the most important in Brazil*
mais importante do que Liverpool *more important than Liverpool*
você vê? *can you see?*
todos *all*
barcos (os) *boats*
vêm *come*
toda parte *every part*
mundo (o) *world*
incrível *incredible*
diga uma coisa *tell me something*
alunos (os) *pupils*
mais ou menos *more or less*
come *you eat*
durante *during*
refeitório (o) *canteen*
almoço/almoço (o) *I lunch/lunch*
bem perto *really near*
a que horas *at what time*
começa/começo *you/I begin*
saio *I leave/go out*
às vezes *sometimes*

turma (a) *class/group*
tanto trabalho *so much work*
é mesmo *you're right/it really is/sure thing*

Exercise 1

Choose the correct words to fill in the gaps.

a Santos é um porto muito _____ grande/pequeno.
b Marli come o almoço _____ num restaurante/num café.
c Marli trabalha _____ muito/pouco.

_____

Grammar

O mais importante *The most important*

When making comparisons between things, places or people, Portuguese uses **mais** more or **menos** less. The structure is: **X é mais (menos) ADJECTIVE do que Y**. For example:

Santos é mais importante do que Liverpool.

Often in spoken Portuguese, the **do que** becomes just **que**. The superlative (i.e. the highest degree) of these comparisons is expressed as: **X é o/a (_____) mais ADJECTIVE**. For example:

Santos é o (porto) mais importante. *Santos is the most important (port).*

Some adjectives have slightly irregular forms of comparison. Look at the table below.

Adjective	Comparative	Superlative
alto *tall*	**mais alto** *taller*	**o mais alto** *the tallest*
grande *big*	**maior** *bigger*	**o maior** *the biggest*
		(Contd)

Adjective	Comparative	Superlative
pequeno small	**menor** smaller	**o menor** the smallest
bom good	**melhor** better	**o melhor** the best
mau bad	**pior** worse	**o pior** the worst

Study these examples:

José é mais alto do que Marli. *José is taller than Marli.*
O tempo hoje está melhor. *The weather today is better.*
Ela é a pior* aluna. *She is the worst pupil.*

Pior and **melhor** are typically placed before the noun.

More verbs

In Unit 2 you learnt how to use all the parts of the **-ar** verb
trabalhar. To talk about daily routines you need to know how to
form verbs from the other two main groups.

	-er **comer** to eat	-ir **partir** to leave
eu	com**o**	part**o**
ele/ela	com**e**	part**e**
você	com**e**	part**e**
nós	com**emos**	part**imos**
eles/elas	com**em**	part**em**
vocês	com**em**	part**em**

You will see that the endings for these two groups are very
similar.

Ver, vir *To see, to come*

Irregular verbs are always awkward, and you must concentrate
hard in order to learn them adequately. Two verbs most commonly

mixed up are **ver** and **vir**. Look at the two of them in the present tense.

ver *to see*	vir *to come*
vejo	**venho**
vê	**vem**
vemos	**vimos**
veem	**vêm**

Todo, todas *All, every*

Todo is an adjective meaning *all/every*, and has four parts agreeing with what it is describing.

todo	toda	todos	todas

You will also come across **tudo**. This is a neuter word (neither m nor f) meaning *everything/all that*, which is non-specific. It never changes form.

todo (o) dia/todos os dias	*every day*
todas as pessoas	*all the people/everyone*
tudo é bom	*everything is good*

The numbers game 100–1000

Here are some more numbers for you to learn.

101	cento e um, uma	150	cento e cinquenta
102	cento e dois, duas	160	cento e sessenta
105	cento e cinco	170	cento e setenta
110	cento e dez	180	cento e oitenta
120	cento e vinte	190	cento e noventa
130	cento e trinta	199	cento e noventa e nove
140	cento e quarenta		

These are on the recording.

◆) CD1, TR 6, 01:46

100	cem	600	seiscentos/as
200	duzentos/as	700	setecentos/as
300	trezentos/as	800	oitocentos/as
400	quatrocentos/as	900	novecentos/as
500	quinhentos/as	1.000	mil

Use the feminine form of these numbers if you are discussing feminine items, e.g. **trezentas milhas** (*300 miles*). Hundreds, tens and units are each divided by **e**. After thousands there is no **e**, except if the thousand if followed by 1–100, or when followed by 200–999 if the last two numbers are zeros.

1056 – mil e	*2300 – dois mil e*	*4897 – quatro mil,*
cinquenta e seis	**trezentos**	**oitocentos e noventa**
		e sete

Insight

Take your time learning the numbers, but try to take every opportunity to practise them in your everyday routines: shopping, lottery, car registrations. Train your mind to see the numeral and instantly put it into Portuguese. It happens in time.

Time

Saying at what time things happen is not much different from what you learnt in the previous unit.

às ... (horas)	*at ... (o' clock)*
às ... e ...	*at ... (minutes past)*
às ... para ...	*at ... to ...*
à uma hora	*at one o' clock*
ao meio dia/à meia-noite	*at midday/midnight*

Look at these examples:

às cinco horas	*at five o' clock*
às dez e vinte	*at 10.20*
às quinze para as oito	*at 7.45*

Dialogue 2

José asks Sylvia about her daily routine.

José	Sylvia, você mora mesmo em Manchester?
Sylvia	Bem, moro a cinco quilômetros de Manchester, numa pequena aldeia, mas trabalho em Manchester.
José	Como é que você vai ao trabalho? Vai de carro?
Sylvia	Não, de manhã e à tarde o trânsito é impossível, por isso vou de bicicleta no verão. Saio de casa às oito e chego ao trabalho às oito e meia.
José	E no inverno – também vai de bicicleta no frio?
Sylvia	Não, não tenho coragem – em Manchester chove muito no inverno. Ou vou de ônibus, ou pego uma carona com uma amiga.
José	A que horas sai do escritório à tarde?
Sylvia	Em geral saio de lá por volta das cinco e meia, mas às vezes fico trabalhando até às seis, seis e um pouco.

QUICK VOCAB

mesmo em Manchester *in Manchester itself/right in Manchester*
a 5 quilômetros de *5 km from*
aldeia (a) *village*
como vai a …? *how do you get to …?*
de carro/bicicleta/ônibus *by car/bike/bus*
trânsito (o) *traffic*
impossível *impossible*
por isso *for that reason/so*
verão (o) *summer*
chego *I arrive*

inverno (o) *winter*
coragem (a) *courage*
ou ... ou ... *either ... or ...*
pego uma carona *I get a lift*
amiga (a) *friend*
escritório (o) *office*
em geral *generally*
por volta de *around*
às vezes *sometimes*
fico trabalhando *I stay working*

Exercise 2

Say if these statements are **verdadeiro** or **falso**.

                                                             V   F

  a Sylvia lives in Manchester itself.
  b In summer she cycles to work.
  c Sometimes she works until 9 pm.

Grammar

> ### Insight
> **... é que ...?** *... is it that ...?*
>
> Often, the expression **é que** (*is it that*) is inserted into a
> question to either emphasize something important, or simply
> to enhance the flow of the sentence. If you have studied
> French, you will recognize the expression **est-ce que**. **Onde é
> que você trabalha?** *Where is it that you work?*

Transport

To talk about means of transport, you use a verb (usually **ir** – *to go*),
plus **de** plus the transport. There are a couple of exceptions. The
following table contains some examples.

$$\text{de} \begin{cases} \textbf{carro} \; car \\ \textbf{ônibus} \; bus \\ \textbf{bicicleta} \; bicycle \\ \textbf{ônibus (de luxo)} \; coach \\ \textbf{metrô} \; underground \\ \textbf{motocicleta} \; motorbike \\ \textbf{avião} \; aeroplane \\ \textbf{trem} \; train \\ \textbf{barco} \; boat \end{cases} \qquad \text{a} \begin{cases} \textbf{cavalo} \; horse \\ \textbf{pé} \; foot \end{cases}$$

Two irregular verbs – **pedir/sair**

These two verbs have certain irregularities, so be careful when using them. In the present tense they are:

pedir	to ask for	sair	to go out
peço		saio	
pede		sai	
pedimos		saímos	
pedem		saem	

Test yourself

é o/a mais ... de ...	*it's the most ... in the ...*
é mais/menos ... (do/ de) que ...	*it's more/less ... than ...*
a que horas começa/termina?	*at what time do you start/finish?*
começo/termino às ...	*I start/finish at ...*
ao meio dia/à meia noite	*at midday/midnight*
(você) mora em ...?	*do you live in ...?*
como vai ao trabalho?	*how do you get to work?*
vou de carro/bicicleta/táxi	*I go by car/bicycle/taxi*
saio por volta das ...	*I leave about ... o'clock*
fico trabalhando até ...	*I stay/remain working until ...*

Practice

◆) CD1, TR 6, 02:20

1 Look at the following extract from Nelson's diary, then listen to him describing his daily routine and fill in the gaps in his diary with activities or times, as though he has written it himself.

8.15	a ?
8.50	*chego ao trabalho*
9.00	b ?
10.00	
c ?	*como o almoço*
d ?	
17.35	
e ?	*chego em casa*

2 Fill in the gaps with appropriate times.

a Sónia sai de casa _____

b Miguel vai ao trabalho _____

c Ana pega o ônibus _____

d Eu saio da escola _____

e José come o almoço _____

f Sylvia chega em casa _____

3 Make sentences describing where places are in relation to each other, writing out in Portuguese the distances.

   a [Portugal] é a [600 km] da [France].
   b [Brazil] é a [1896 km] do [Mexico].
   c [England] é a [1247 km] de [Portugal].
   d [USA] são a [6,125 km] da [Argentina].

4 Match the questions with the answers.

   a Como vai ao trabalho?
   b Quantas pessoas trabalham lá?
   c Você mora em Londres?
   d A que horas come o almoço?
   e Você come no escritório?

   i Mais ou menos 120.
   ii Ao meio-dia.
   iii Vou de ônibus.
   iv Não, vou a um café.
   v Não, moro em Manchester.

Testing yourself – do you understand?

People do all kinds of work. Look at these advertisements overleaf, and see if you can answer these questions.

1 Luci is a fortune-teller – true or false?
2 What language must you speak to get the au pair's job?
3 Which advertisement would you answer if you needed some sewing doing?
4 Who can help you if you are suffering from stress?
5 The 26-year-old Brazilian girl would like to be a teacher – true or false?
6 Where might you apply for a job if you enjoyed driving?

6

O que faz no tempo livre?
What do you do in your free time?

In this unit you will learn
- *How to talk about leisure time*
- *How to discuss what you like doing*
- *How to talk about leisure facilities and entertainment*

Dialogue 1

Sylvia and the Ferreiras discuss their favourite leisure activities.

José	Sylvia, o que você faz no seu tempo livre?	
Sylvia	Adoro ler. Durante a semana, quando volto do trabalho, gosto muito de escutar um pouco de música, e ler um bom livro.	
José	Que tipo de livros prefere?	
Sylvia	Prefiro os livros policiais, mas também leio muitos jornais.	
Marli	E qual é a música de que você gosta mais?	
Sylvia	Gosto da música latina, mas para relaxar ouço música clássica.	
Marli	Vai adorar a música popular brasileira – é ótima para dançar.	
Sylvia	Vocês, o que fazem nas horas vagas?	
	(Contd)	

CD1, TR 7, 00:09

José	Aos fins de semana costumamos passar tempo no clube — nadando, jogando tênis, relaxando no bar. Pessoalmente gosto de jogar golfe, mas Marli não gosta.
Marli	É verdade, eu prefiro fazer cooper bem cedo de manhã, e aos domingos pratico ioga.
Sylvia	E a televisão? As famosas telenovelas brasileiras?
Marli	Só quando não temos mais nada a fazer.

o que você/s faz/em? *what do you* (sing/pl) *do?*
o tempo livre/as horas vagas *free/leisure time*
adoro/gosto *I love/like*
ler *to read*
quando *when*
volto/leio/ouço *I return/read/listen*
ouvir/escutar *to hear/listen to*
a música latina/clássica *Latin/classical music*
a música popular brasileira *Brazilian pop music*
livro (o) *book*
que tipo de *what kind of*
prefere/prefiro *s/he prefers, you prefer/I prefer*
livros policiais (os) *crime novels*
jornais (os) *newspapers*
relaxar/dançar *to relax/dance*
vai adorar *you're going to love*
ótimo/a *great*
aos fins de semana *at weekends*
aos domingos *on Sundays*
costumamos *we usually/we are accustomed to*
passar tempo *to spend time*
clube (o) *social club*
nadando/relaxando *swimming/relaxing*
jogando tênis *playing tennis*
bar (o) *bar*
pessoalmente *personally*
não gosta *s/he does not like*
golfe (o) *golf*
é verdade *it's true*
fazer cooper *to go jogging*

bem cedo *really early*
pratico ioga *I do yoga*
televisão (a) *TV*
as famosas telenovelas brasileiras *the famous Brazilian*
 soap operas
mais nada a fazer *nothing else to do*

Exercise

Say which activities the characters from the dialogue do and don't like doing.

		reading	sports	television	music
a	Marli				
b	José				
c	Sylvia				

Grammar

Activity vocabulary

Here are some words you will find useful in order to discuss leisure activities.

Verbs

jogar tênis/futebol/vôlei/golfe *to play tennis/football/volleyball/golf*
passear *to go strolling*
correr/fazer cooper *to run/go jogging*
pintar *to paint*
ler livros/revistas/jornais *to read books/magazines/newspapers*
escutar música *to listen to music*
nadar *to swim*
assistir um show/um jogo *to go to a show/a game*
ir a... *to go to...*

Nouns

a piscina *swimming pool*
o clube *social/sports club*
o museu *museum*
o rádio/a TV *radio/TV*
o centro esportivo *sports centre*
o cinema *cinema*
o teatro *theatre*
o campo *countryside*
o estádio *sports/football stadium*

Likes/dislikes/preferences

Some important verbs to express your likes and dislikes are:

gostar (de) *to like*
não gostar (de) *to not like*
adorar *to adore*
detestar *to detest*
preferir *to prefer*
gostar mais (de) *to like most/more*

When talking about activities, all these verbs are followed by an infinitive (remember, that is the part of the verb ending in -r which you will find in the dictionary). Be careful with the *I* person of preferir: it is **prefiro**. For example:

Prefiro ler.	*I prefer reading/to read.*
Adoro jogar golfe.	*I love playing/to play golf.*
Lúcia prefere ver televisão.	*Lucia prefers to watch/watching TV.*
João gosta mais de nadar.	*John likes to swim/swimming most.*

Gostar (de) *To like*

Gostar is always followed by **de**. If the verb is used with a noun, you must remember to combine the **de** with words like **o, a, um, uma** etc. if appropriate. For example:

Gostamos de pintar.	*We like to paint/painting.*
Gosto do sol.	*I like the sun.*
Ele gosta mais da cerveja.	*He likes the beer most.*

The '**de**' is left out when the verb is used on its own, for example, as an answer to a question: **você gosta de vinho? Sim, gosto.** *Do you like wine? Yes I do (like it).*

Irregular plurals

Nouns and adjectives which end in **-l** in the singular have irregular endings, as you saw in the dialogue:

o jornal – jorn*ais*
policial – polici*ais*

Be on the look-out for others as you develop your reading skills.

More irregular verbs

Some more important verbs with irregularities.

fazer *to do, make*	**ler** *to read*	**ouvir** *to hear*
faço	leio	ouço
faz	lê	ouve
fazemos	lemos	ouvimos
fazem	leem	ouvem

Time routines

◄๏ **CD1, TR 7, 01:56**

The days of the week are:

segunda-feira	*Monday*	**sexta-feira**	*Friday*
terça-feira	*Tuesday*	**sábado**	*Saturday*
quarta-feira	*Wednesday*	**domingo**	*Sunday*
quinta-feira	*Thursday*		

To say when you do certain activities, you can say:

aos (nos) sábados/aos (nos)	*on Saturdays/Sundays/at the*
domingos/ao (no) fim de semana	*weekend*
às (nas) segundas, terças, etc.	*on Mondays, Tuesdays, etc.*
todos/as os/as	*every (lit. all the…)*
todos os sábados	*every Saturday*
cada	*each, every*
cada quinta	*every Thursday*

-ando *-ing*

The Portuguese equivalent of the *-ing* form of verbs is formed thus:
verb in infinitive minus the ending (**-ar/-er/-ir**) + **-ando/-endo/-indo**.
For example:

escutar *to listen (to)* **escut-** + **-ando** = **escutando** *listening to*

Ele prefere ficar em casa	*He prefers to stay at home*
escutando música.	*listening to music.*

BUT to say *I like swimming* you must still use the structure
mentioned earlier with the verb to like – **gostar de/adorar** +
infinitive, e.g. **gosto de nadar** *I like to swim/swimming*.

Dialogue 2

The Ferreiras take Sylvia out to a local bar.

José	Quer provar uma bebida nacional, Sylvia?
Sylvia	O que é?
José	É caipirinha. Sabe o que é?
Sylvia	Não faço ideia.
Marli	É uma delícia – feita de cachaça, um aguardente de cana de açúcar, com limão, açúcar e água. É um bocado forte.
Sylvia	Então, por que não?
José	Garçom, por favor.
Garçom	Pois não?
José	Duas caipirinhas e uma batida de morango.
Garçom	Muito bem.
Marli	Sylvia, você vai ao teatro em Manchester?
Sylvia	De vez em quando sim. Prefiro ir ao cinema quando surge a oportunidade. Há bons teatros aqui?
Marli	Ah, sim, aqui em São Paulo há muitos – cinemas e teatros com todo tipo de peça – comédia/romance/musical – só que em alguns os ingressos são bastante caros.
José	Em São Paulo há coisas para todo mundo – cinema, teatro, museu, discoteca, galeria de arte – há de tudo.

quer provar? *do you want to try?*
bebida (a) *drink*
nacional *national*
o que é? *what is it?*
caipirinha (a) *sugar cane/lime drink*
não faço ideia *I've no idea*
uma delícia *delicious (a delight)*
cachaça (a), aguardente (o) *firewater*
limão (o) *lime*
água (a) *water*
um bocado forte *a bit strong*
pois não? *can I help you?*
uma batida de morango *a strawberry/wine cocktail*
quando surge a oportunidade *when the opportunity arises*
de vez em quando *sometimes*
peça (a) *play*
ingressos (os) *tickets*

caro/a *expensive*
todo mundo *everyone*
discoteca (a) *disco*
há de tudo *there's a bit of everything*

True or false?

Are the following sentences **verdadeiras** or **falsas**?

	V	F

a Caipirinha is an alcoholic drink.
b Sylvia never goes to the theatre.
c São Paulo has a wide range of activities.

Grammar

> ### Insight
> When asking someone if they would like something, you can
> either say **quer** (lit. *do you want?*), or **queria** (*would you like?*).
> Despite the latter being considered more polite in English, it
> is not considered rude to use **quer**, and is common practice
> throughout Brazil.

Here are the two forms in full:

quero	*I want*	**queria**	*I would like*
quer	*you, s/he/it want(s)*	**queria**	*you would like, he, she, etc.*
queremos	*we want*	**queríamos**	*we would like*
querem	*you/they want*	**queriam**	*you/they would like*

'To know' or 'to know'?

There are two verbs for to know in Portuguese – **saber** is *to know a fact* or *how to do something*; **conhecer** is *to know a person, place* and *to meet, get to know someone*.

sei	conheço
sabe	conhece
sabemos	conhecemos
sabem	conhecem

e.g. **Que horas são? Não sei.** *What time is it? I don't know.*
Maria sabe andar a cavalo. *Maria knows how to ride a horse.*
Ela conhece meu filho. *She knows my son.*
Ainda não conheço Brasília. *I do not know Brasilia yet.*

Some ...

The full version is:

> algum   alguma   alguns   algumas

You can also use:

> um   uma   uns   umas

Algum, etc. can be contracted with **em** (*in*, *on*) (**nalgum**) and **de** (*of*, *from*) (**dalgum**), although you will rarely come across these forms in Brazil.

Study these examples:

Algumas (umas) pessoas trabalham muito. *Some people work a lot.*

Não gosto de entrar em alguns (nalguns) bares. *I don't like going in to some bars.*

Insight

Many alcoholic drinks in Brazil take as their base the delicious tropical fruits available there. **Batidas** are cocktails of wine, red or white, blended with a fruit – favourites are **batida de coco** *coconut*, **morango** *strawberry*, **maracujá** *passion fruit*, **pêssego** *peach*. **Caipirinha** is very potent and easily addictive! Lime and sugar are mixed with firewater,

(Contd)

commonly referred to as **pinga** or **cachaça,** and is extremely easy to drink in copious amounts. Be careful – it has a kick! During the February carnival many people take to the streets with cans filled with pure pinga tied around their necks. No wonder they keep the samba going for five days!

Test yourself

o que faz/em no seu tempo livre/horas vagas?	*what do you do in your free leisure time?*
gosto muito de ler/escutar música	*I like reading/listening to music a lot*
que prefere?	*what do you prefer?*
prefiro ...	*I prefer ...*
costumo/costumamos ...	*I/we usually ...*
aos domingos/às segundas	*on Sundays/Mondays*
você vai ao teatro/cinema?	*do you go to the theatre/cinema?*
de vez em quando/às vezes	*sometimes*
há bons teatros/museus aqui?	*are there any good theatres/museums here?*
há de tudo	*there's a bit of everything*

Practice

1 Link up the pictures of the activities with what the bubbles are describing.

i Gosto de visitar o museu

ii Paulo adora jogar tênis

iii Gostamos muito de ouvir música

iv Ana prefere ler

v Adoro nadar

2 Saber or conhecer?

Place the correct form of the appropriate verb in the spaces.

a Eu _____ a França muito bem.
b Miguel não _____ nadar.
c A que horas vamos ao cinema? Eu não _____.
d Sônia, você _____ Senhor Veloso?
e Eles não _____ esta cidade.

◄» **CD1, TR 7, 03:45**

3 Listen to three people (speakers 1, 2 and 3) discussing what they like doing in their leisure time, and decide which profile below belongs to which person.

a likes painting, museums and playing golf
b prefers watching TV, doesn't like sports
c likes golf and tennis but doesn't like music

4 Fill in your part of the dialogue about leisure time.

Francisco	O que você faz no seu tempo livre?
You	*(Say I love swimming, I go to the swimming pool on Saturdays.)*
Francisco	E você gosta de música?
You	*(Say yes, a little.)*
Francisco	Que tipo de música prefere?
You	*(Say I prefer jazz. Ask Francisco what he does in his free time.)*
	(Contd)

Testing yourself – do you understand?

1 Below is some information about courses you can do at a local college. Paulo has chosen a course on gardening. Look at how he has filled in his request form overleaf, then choose a course yourself, and fill in the blank form that follows with personal details.

Electrônica básica radiotécnica e (áudio televisão p.b. e em cores)		Silk-screen	Golfe	Espanhol
		Desenho artístico e publicitário	Violão	Mecânica de automóveis
Corte e costura	Fotografia	Eletricidade	Eletricidade de automóveis	Auxiliar de escritório
Auxiliar de contabilidade	Auxiliar em administração de empresas	Tricô	Bordado e crochê	Beleza de mulher
Secretariado moderno	Jardinagem	Vinhos	Mestre de obras (edificações)	Natação
Mecânica geral	Mecânica de motos	Refrigeração e ar condicionado	Desenho de mecânica	Desenho arquitetônico
Especialização em gravação digital	Técnicas vendas	Informática	Inglês	Caligrafia

```
┌─────────────────────────────────────────────────────────┐
│           INSTITUTO UNIVERSAL BRASILEIRO SP               │
│  Av. Rio Branco, 781 – Caixa Postal 5058 – São Paulo – CEP 01061-970 │
│                                                           │
│  Sr. Diretor, peço Grátis o folheto sobre o(s) curso(s) profissionalizante(s) │
│  livre(s) de   _Jardinagem_  ◄──────────────────── COURSE │
│                                                           │
│  NOME   _Paulo de Oliveira Martins_                       │
│                                                           │
│  RUA  _Julieta Mesquita_                      Nº _35_     │
│                                                           │
│  CEP _01326_        BAIRRO _Centro_   CX. POSTAL ____  ◄── MAIL BOX No. │
│                                                           │
│  CIDADE _Belo Horizonte_   ESTADO _Minas_                 │
└─────────────────────────────────────────────────────────┘
```

POST CODE → CEP

DISTRICT → BAIRRO

```
┌─────────────────────────────────────────────────────────┐
│           INSTITUTO UNIVERSAL BRASILEIRO SP               │
│  Av. Rio Branco, 781 – Caixa Postal 5058 – São Paulo – CEP 01061-970 │
│                                                           │
│  Sr. Diretor, peço Grátis o folheto sobre o(s) curso(s) profissionalizante(s) │
│  livre(s) de  _____     │
│                                                           │
│  NOME  _____   │
│                                                           │
│  RUA  _____  Nº ____  │
│                                                           │
│  CEP _____  BAIRRO _____  CX. POSTAL _____  │
│                                                           │
│  CIDADE _____  ESTADO _____    │
└─────────────────────────────────────────────────────────┘
```

2 Which courses would you choose if you wanted to study:
  a The guitar
  b General mechanics
  c Art and design

7

Pois não?
Can I help you?

In this unit you will learn
- *How to obtain goods and services*
- *How to buy clothes and shoes*
- *How to discuss sizes*

Dialogue 1

Sylvia has gone to visit Rio and decides to do some shopping in a fashion store (**a boutique**) before starting her journey northwards.

CD1, TR 8, 00:07

Empregada	Pois não?
Sylvia	Queria ver umas camisetas, por favor.
Empregada	Claro. Qual é o seu tamanho?
Sylvia	É o 42.
Empregada	Você procura uma cor em particular?
Sylvia	Tem em verde, ou azul?
Empregada	Sim, temos estas aqui, e também aquelas ali em outro estilo. São todas de algodão.
Sylvia	Posso provar?
Empregada	Claro – a cabine de provas é ali ao fundo. *(Sylvia comes out of the changing room.)*
Empregada	Então, já escolheu?
Sylvia	Acho que sim. Vou levar esta azul, mas tem a outra em verde-escuro?

Empregada	Neste momento não, sinto muito.
Sylvia	Não faz mal. Levo as duas. Quanto é?
Empregada	São 36 reais ao todo. Quer pagar ali na caixa? Leve este talão consigo. Depois volte aqui para pegar as camisetas.
Sylvia	Obrigada.

QUICK VOCAB

Pois não? *Can I help you?*
camisetas (as) *t-shirts*
claro *of course*
tamanho (o) *size*
você procura ...? *are you looking for ...?*
uma cor em particular *a particular colour*
estilo (o) *style*
posso provar? *may I try (it) on?*
cabine de provas (a) *changing room*
ao fundo *at the bottom, end*
já escolheu? *have you chosen yet?*
acho que sim *I think so*
vou levar *I'll take*
neste momento *at the moment*
sinto muito *I'm sorry*
não faz mal *that's OK*
quanto é? *how much is it/that?*
ao todo *in all*
pagar *to pay for*
caixa (a) *till/check-out*
leve/volte *take/return*
talão (o) *ticket/stub*
consigo *with you*

Exercise 1

Only one of these statements is true. Which one?

a O tamanho da Sylvia é quarenta e quatro.
b A cabine de provas é à esquerda.
c Sylvia leva duas camisetas.

Grammar

Posso ...? *May I ...?*

Posso *may I/can I* can be used with all kinds of verbs in the infinitive, and is very useful. **Posso ver?** *May I see, have a look?* **Posso experimentar, provar?** *Can I try on, try something, taste?* **Posso passar?** *May I pass, get by?* The verb is **poder** *to be able to* and in full is:

posso	**podemos**
pode	**podem**

I think so

The verb **achar** has various meanings *to find, think, reckon.* It can be used when asking/giving opinions:

Acho que sim/não.	*I think so/not.*
O que você acha?	*What do you think?*
Acho muito bonito.	*I think (it's) very pretty.*

You can also use **creio que** *I believe (that)* and **penso que** *I think (that).*

In English we often say things like 'I think I'll go...', but in Portuguese you have to remember to say 'I think THAT I'll go...'. **Penso QUE vou...**

Levo *I'll take*

Levo is in fact the present tense of the verb even though in English we are saying *I will take* (i.e. future). This replacement of a future action with a verb in the present tense is very common in Portuguese, especially in spoken dialogue. For example:

Amanhã vejo meu irmão.	*Tomorrow I'll see my brother.*
Falamos a semana que vem.	*We'll talk next week.*

As in English, you can also use the verb *to go* (**ir**) to express future action. For example:

Vou à cidade amanhã.   *I'm going to town tomorrow.*

The future tense will be introduced later in the course.

Leve…, volte …: *commands*

In Unit 4, you learnt how to give directions, politely telling people what to do by saying you *(do) this/that*. There are also other ways of ordering people to do things more directly. These are called *commands*, or more technically *imperatives*. Remember that you do not need to be annoyed with someone in order to tell them to do or not do something. To form the commands, look at the following steps:

-ar verbs: **comprar**	-er verbs: **comer**	-ir verbs: **partir**
(você) **compra** = *you buy*	**come** = *you eat*	**parte** = *you leave*

To form the command change the verb endings to the following:

compre! = *buy!*   **coma!** = *eat!*   **parta!** = *leave!*

There is a crossing-over of endings – the **-ar** verbs take an **-e**, and the **-er/-ir** verbs take an **-a**. To command more than one person, add an **-m**. For example:

(vocês) **comprem!**   **comam!**   **partam!**

To tell somebody not to do something, simply place **não** in front – **não coma!** *don't eat!* Be careful with irregular verbs: here is a small selection of some you have already come across:

	Sing. Command	Pl. command
Fazer *to do, make*	**faça!**	**façam!**
Ver *to see*	**veja!**	**vejam!**

(Contd)

	Sing. Command	Pl. command
Ir *to go*	**vá!**	**vão!**
Vir *to come*	**venha!**	**venham!**
Pedir *to ask for*	**peça!**	**peçam!**

Insight

Be on the look-out for irregular verbs, but don't expect to take them on board all at once. They are particularly tricky in Portuguese, and take time to learn.

Dialogue 2

Sylvia next goes to a shoe shop – **a sapataria**.

CD1, TR 8, 01:27

Sylvia	Bom dia. Queria ver uns sapatos em couro, por favor. Tem?
Empregada	Sim, temos. Que número é que você calça?
Sylvia	Acho que é o 38, mas não tenho certeza.
Empregada	Bom, em 38 temos estes, que estão muito na moda agora.
Sylvia	Sim, são muito bonitos, mas queria alguma coisa mais resistente – para andar.
Empregada	Temos estas botas, que são cómodas, e estão em liquidação esta semana.
Sylvia	Posso experimentar?
Empregada	Claro. Tome!
Sylvia	São muito pequenas. Tem outras maiores?
Empregada	Sim, aqui em 39.
Sylvia	Ah, sim, estas são mais cómodas. O que você acha?
Empregada	Apesar de ser resistentes, também é 'chique'. Ficam-lhe bem.
Sylvia	Quanto custam?
Empregada	Com o desconto, custam 85 reais.
Sylvia	Que pechincha!

sapatos (os) *shoes*
couro (o) *leather*
tem? *do you have?*
que número ... calça? *what size do you take?*
não tenho certeza *I'm not sure*
estar na moda *to be in fashion*
resistente *solid/firm*
andar *to walk*
botas (as) *boots*
cómodas *comfortable*
em liquidação *in the sale*
são muito pequenas *they're too (very) small*
apesar de ser *in spite of being*
chique *chic*
ficam-lhe bem *they suit you*
quanto custa/m *how much does it/do they cost?*
desconto (o) *discount*
que pechincha *what a bargain*

Exercise 2

Answer three questions in Portuguese, based on the dialogue.

  a O que a Sylvia quer comprar? _____
  b Qual é o número das botas que ela compra? _____
  c Quanto custam? _____

_____

Grammar

Clothes check-list

a blusa *blouse*	**a camisa** *shirt*
a calça *trousers*	**o vestido** *dress*
a saia *skirt*	**as cuecas** *underpants*
as calcinhas *knickers*	**o sutiã** *bra*
as meias *socks*	**as sandálias** *sandals*
as luvas *gloves*	**o chapéu** *hat*

Materials

algodão cotton	**poliéster** polyester
couro leather	**plástico** plastic
lã wool	**seda** silk
cetim satin	**malha** jersey/knitwear
linho linen	**fibras sintéticas** synthetic fibres

Shops

Often the name of a shop is derived from the item sold there.

sapatos shoes	**sapataria** shoe shop
pão bread	**padaria** baker's
livro book	**livraria** book shop
pastel pastry, cake	**pastelaria** cake shop
tabaco tobacco	**tabacaria** tobacconist's
fruta fruit	**frutaria** fruiterer
bilhete ticket	**bilheteria** ticket office

Test yourself

Queria/posso ... ver/provar/ experimentar?	*I woud like to/may I ... see/try on/try?*
Qual tamanho/que número calça?	*What size/ What size shoe do you take?*
Em que cor?	*In which colour?*
Tem .../tem em ...?	*Do you have/do you have in ...?*
Quanto é/quanto custa/m?	*How much is it/does it/they cost?*
Levo/vou levar	*I'll take/I'm going to take*
Acho que	*I think that*
É/são muito pequeno/s, grande/s	*It is/they are too small/large*
Fica/m-lhe bem	*It suits/they suit you*

....

Insight

Rio is a city of great contrasts. It is arguably one of the most
beautiful cities in the world, with its breathtaking scenery
and renowned beaches. But there is also great poverty in the

shantytowns (**as favelas**). Many will have heard of the police death squads hired by business people to rid the streets of the children who sleep rough. Rio is everything from squalor to extravagance, but it all comes together for its magnificent February carnival – **o carnaval**. Do be careful in Rio – exercise caution when out and about, but don't be too afraid to enjoy its beauty. And don't be shocked by the amount of flesh shown on the beach. Brazilian women don't often sunbathe topless, but their bikinis reveal an awful lot of flesh. Often referred to as '**fio dental**' bikinis *(dental floss!)*, they leave little to the imagination. Tone up before you venture on to Copacabana, Ipanema and Leblon!

Practice

1 Match up the items to be bought with the appropriate shops. You may wish to look back to Unit 4 to refresh your memory.

| **i** livraria | **ii** sapataria | **iii** mercado | **iv** açougue |
| | **v** boutique | **vi** padaria | |

2 Supply your part of the dialogue in a fashion store

You	*(Say do you have skirts?)*
Empregada	Sim, temos. Qual é seu tamanho?
You	*(Say I think it's 42.)*
Empregada	Temos estas, em vermelho e preto.
You	*(Say do you have it in light-blue?)*
Empregada	Sim, temos esta, em outro estilo.
	(Contd)

You	*(Ask how much it is?)*
Empregada	Esta custa 46 reais
You	*(Say I'll take this one in blue and that one in black.)*
Empregada	São 92 reais ao todo.
You	*(Say thank you.)*

3 Fill in the gaps by supplying the correct command form of the verb. Then say what each one means.
   a (você) [comprar] _____ a blusa! _____
   b (vocês) [comer] _____ o pão! _____
   c (vocês) [ir] _____ por aqui! _____
   d (você) [não fazer] _____ barulho! _____
   e (você) [trabalhar] _____ bem! _____
   f (vocês) [não falar] _____ muito! _____

◀) **CD1, TR 8, 02:41**

4 Listen to someone in a shoe shop, and tick the appropriate pictures for their purchases.

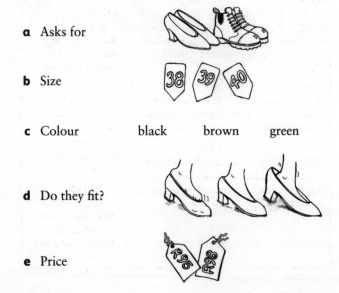

   a Asks for

   b Size

   c Colour   black   brown   green

   d Do they fit?

   e Price

Testing yourself – do you understand?

Look at the advice given to people under their horoscope and answer the following:

a What should Pisces be eating?
b What culinary advice is given to Cancer?
c What should Libra do for their friends?
d What should Capricorn do on arriving home?
e What should Aries do before taking a decision?
f What should Leo treat themselves to?

HORÓSCOPO

PREVISÕES PARA O PERÍODO DE 28 DE DEZEMBRO A 28 DE JANEIRO

CAPRICÓRNIO
22 DEZ. a 20 JAN.
Dica: Quando chegar em casa tome um bom banho de sais.

AQUÁRIO
21 JAN. a 19 FEV.
Dica: Que tal um novo corte de cabelo? Você vai se sentir outra …

PEIXES
20 FEV. a 20 MAR.
Dica: Abuse das saladas. Elas irão manter seu bom humor no verão.

ÁRIES
21 MAR. a 20 ABRIL
Dica: Relaxe muito antes de tomar qualquer decisão.

TOURO
21 ABRIL a 20 MAIO
Dica: Gente. Isso é tudo o que você precisa para melhorar sua vida.

GÊMEOS
21 MAIO a 20 JUNHO
Dica: Não fique apenas pensando em cursos. Faça a matrícula já!

CÂNCER
21 JUNHO a 21 JULHO
Dica: Troque os doces por frutas. Seus dentes vão agradecer.

LEÃO
22 JULHO a 22 AGO.
Dica: Procure uma boa mão oriental e entregue-se às massagens.

VIRGEM
23 AGO. a 22 SET.
Dica: Aposte nos melhores produtos de beleza. Eles vão te ajudar.

LIBRA
23 SET. a 22 OUT.
Dica: Faça um jantar para os seus amigos e ponha um sorriso no rosto, menina.

ESCORPIÃO
23 OUT. a 21 NOV.
Dica: O sol chegou! Aproveite para colocar o bronzeado em dia também.

SAGITÁRIO
22 NOV. a 21 DEZ.
Dica: Viagens à vista. Não tenha medo. Arrume as malas para voar linda.

8

Que vai comer?
What are you going to eat?

In this unit you will learn
- *How to order a meal*
- *More about making requests*
- *About typical Brazilian food*

___

Dialogue 1

Sylvia goes out to a restaurant with a friend.

Márcia	Tem uma mesa livre?
Garçom	São quantos?
Márcia	Somos só dois.
Garçom	Temos esta mesa aqui perto da porta, ou aquela ali ao fundo.
Márcia	Esta está bem. Traga o cardápio por favor.
Garçom	Tome.
Márcia	Deixe ver. O que temos? Há saladas e sopas para começar. Que vai pedir, Sylvia?
Sylvia	Não tenho muita fome. Quero uma sopa quentinha.
Márcia	A canja é boa e típica daqui. É feita de galinha.
Sylvia	Então é isto para mim.
Márcia	Eu vou pedir uma salada mista para mim.

mesa (a) *table*
livre *free*
são quantos? *how many of you are there?*
somos ... *there are ... of us*
porta (a) *door*
traga *bring*
cardápio (o) *menu*
tome *here you are/take*
deixe ver *let (me) see*
saladas (as)/salada mista (a) *salads/mixed salad*
sopas (as)/sopa quentinha (a) *soups/hot soup*
para começar *to start with*
não tenho muita fome *I'm not very hungry*
canja (a) *chicken broth*
típica daqui *typical of here*
é feita de *it's made of/from*
galinha (a) *chicken*
é isto para mim *I'll have this*

Exercise 1

Say if these statements are **verdadeiro** or **falso**.

	V	F

a They choose a table near the door.
b Sylvia is really hungry.
c Márcia chooses soup as a starter.

Grammar

Traga! *Bring!*

This command comes from the verb **trazer** *to bring*. In the last unit you were advised to keep a look-out for verbs with irregularities, and here is an example of a verb whose irregularity affects the command-form: Present tense: **trago, traz, trazemos, trazem**. The command becomes **Traga!** *Bring!*

In addition to those listed in Unit 7, other verbs which act in the same way include:

	Present tense	Command
seguir to follow	**sigo segue seguimos seguem**	**siga!**
repetir to repeat	**repito repete repetimos repetem**	**repita!**
dormir to sleep	**durmo dorme dormimos dormem**	**durma!**

Há … *There is/there are …*

This small word which you met in Unit 4 for directions is extremely versatile. It means *there is/there are*, and when used as a question, also means *is there? are there?* It is particularly useful when requesting information about what is available: **o que há?** *what is there?* **(o) que tem?** *what do you have?* is most commonly used in Brazil as an alternative.

Ter *in special expressions*

The verb **ter** (*to have*) is used in certain expressions such as **tenho fome** *I am hungry*: **ter fome** *to be hungry* (literally *to have hunger*).

You will also come across

ter	**sede**	*to be thirsty*
	sono	*to be sleepy/tired*
	calor	*to be hot*
	frio	*to be cold*

You can also use **estar com** + **fome**, **sede**, etc. literally *to be with hunger*, *thirst*, etc.

> ## Insight
> When you hear new expressions with verbs in them, don't panic! If you understand the other key words, you are off to a good start. '**Calor**', for example, is an easy one to remember.

Dialogue 2

The waiter takes the order.

Garçom	Então, já escolheram? Que vão comer?
Sylvia	Para começar, uma salada mista e uma canja.
Garçom	E depois?
Sylvia	Um lombo assado e um filé de peixe frito com batatas fritas, arroz e legumes para dois.
Garçom	E para beber?
Sylvia	Uma garrafa do vinho da casa.
Garçom	Branco ou tinto?
Sylvia	Branco. E traga uma jarra de água também por favor – tenho muita sede.
Garçom	Muito bem.

QUICK VOCAB

já escolheram? *have you (pl.) chosen yet?*
lombo assado (o) *roast pork loin*
filé de peixe frito (o) *fried fish fillet*
batatas fritas (as) *chips*
arroz (o) *rice*
legumes (os) *vegetables*
garrafa (a) *bottle*
o vinho da casa *the house wine*
tinto *red (wine)*
jarra (a) *jug*

Exercise 2

Answer 'yes' or 'no'.

                                                        YES   NO

a Do they order vegetables for both of them?
b Do they ask for red wine?
c Is Sylvia thirsty?

Insight

The word **tinto** (*red*) is only used for red wine. The everyday word for *red* is **vermelho** or **encarnado**.

Dialogue 3

The meal continues.

Márcia	Garçom, por favor!
Garçom	Diga.
Márcia	Pode trazer mais pão e outra jarra de água, por favor?
Garçom	Claro. Vão querer sobremesas?
Sylvia	O que tem?
Garçom	Hoje temos pudim de caramelo, doce de coco, fruta, e sorvete.
Márcia	Que sabores de sorvete tem?
Garçom	Chocolate, morango, baunilha e avelã.
Márcia	Bom, eu quero um sorvete de morango.
Sylvia	Eu vou provar o pudim.
Garçom	E café?
Márcia	Sim, dois cafezinhos.

QUICK VOCAB

pode trazer *can you bring*
mais pão *more bread*
sobremesas (as) *desserts*
hoje *today*
pudim de caramelo (o) *creme caramel*
doce de coco (o) *coconut dessert*
fruta (a) *fruit*

sorvete (o) *ice cream*
sabores (os) *flavours*
chocolate *chocolate*
morango *strawberry*
baunilha *vanilla*
avelã *hazelnut*

Dialogue 4

Paying the bill.

Márcia	A conta, por favor.
Garçom	Aqui está.
Sylvia	Quanto é, Márcia?
Márcia	São 36 reais.
Sylvia	Tome aqui.
Márcia	Imagine! Pago eu! Insisto. Você é minha convidada.
Sylvia	Bom, a próxima vez eu pago. Obrigada. Foi um jantar delicioso. Mas já é tarde. São nove e meia, e amanhã parto para o nordeste.

foi um jantar delicioso *it was a delicious dinner*
conta (a) *bill*
pago eu *I'll pay*
insisto *I insist*
minha convidada *my guest*

a próxima vez *next time*
já é tarde *it's already late*
o nordeste *the northeast*
imagine! *get away/never!*

QUICK VOCAB

Test yourself

Tem uma mesa livre?	*Do you have a table free?*
Traga o cardápio, por favor	*Please bring the menu.*
Que vai pedir/comer?	*What are you going to have/eat?*
O que há/tem? Há/Tem …	*What is there/do you have?* There is …
Tenho fome/sede.	*I'm hungry/thirsty.*
Para começar/e depois/para beber	*For starters/and then/to drink*
Pode trazer mais …/outro/a …	*Can you bring more …/another …*
Que sabores?	*What flavours?*
A conta, por favor.	*The bill please.*
Foi um (jantar) delicioso.	*It was a delicious (dinner).*

Insight

The Brazilians' main staple of food is rice and black beans – **arroz e feijão,** usually eaten with steak **um filé** and chips and salad. You can hear the beans cooking away all day in pressure cookers down many residential streets. When eating out, popular choices include Italian food (there is a huge Italian community in and around São Paulo); chicken (**frango**) and fish (**peixe**). Sunday is the day for the infamous black bean stew cooked with all kinds of sausage and off-cuts – *feijoada.* Sometimes it's better not to enquire what every bit is! It is served with rice, **couve à mineira** (*sautéd greens*) and **farofa** – a breadcrumb mixture (**manioc**), and also a slice of orange to aid digestion. In the south you are more likely to eat in a **churrascaria-rodízio** – a sort of organized barbecue, where waiters circle the tables with swordsful of every meat you can imagine. As your plate empties you simply catch the waiters' attention. There is usually a help-yourself salad bar, and normally you pay one price and eat until you burst. This is particularly popular in the **gaúcho** – cowboy-regions of the south. More about these later in the course.

Meals are leisurely affairs, unless you are working – but even here many a deal has been clinched over an extended lunch.

Typical Brazilian food

Entradas – *starters*

canja *chicken broth*	**lula frita** *fried squid*
creme de aspargos *asparagus soup*	**salada mista** *tomato/lettuce salad*
camarão *prawns*	**salada de palmito** *salad of palm hearts*

Prato principal – *main course*

lombo assado *roast pork loin*	**massa** *pasta*
frango ensopado *chicken stew*	**espeto misto** *mixed kebab*
ovelha *lamb*	**bife na brasa** *barbecued steak*

94

Guarnições – *side dishes*

arroz *rice*
legumes *vegetables*
ervilhas *peas*

batatas fritas *chips*
farofa *manioc mixture*
feijão *beans*

Sobremesas – *desserts*

sorvete *ice cream*
fruta *fruit*

pudim de caramelo *creme caramel*
doce de coco *coconut dessert*

Bebidas – *drinks*

refrigerantes *soft drinks*
cerveja *beer*
suco de fruta *fruit juice*
água *water*

vinho *wine*

Practice

1 Can you do the following?
   a Say do you have a table free?
   b Say there are five of us.
   c Say I'm not thirsty.
   d Ask your friend what s/he is going to have.
   e Call the waiter across.
   f Ask for the bill.

2 Place an appropriate command from the box over the page into the spaces.
   a Para o museu? _____ por esta rua!
   b _____ favor!
   c Não _____ todo o vinho!
   d _____ a frase!
   e Não _____ tão rápido!
   f Por favor, _____ mais água!

traga beba sigam coma falem faça repitam

3 Use the food lists on the previous pages to help you complete your part of this dialogue.

Garçom	Então, já escolheu? Que vai comer?
You	*(Say to start, a vegetable soup.)*
Garçom	E depois?
You	*(Say lamb with rice and salad.)*
Garçom	E para beber?
You	*(Say a beer and a jug of water.)*
Garçom	Muito bem.

◀) **CD1, TR 9, 01:21**

4 Listen to the dialogue about desserts and fill in the gaps with the missing words.

    A Vão querer _____?

    B O que tem?

    A _____ temos fruta, _____, e pudim.

    B Que sabores de sorvete tem?

    A Chocolate, _____, e avelã.

    B Bom, eu quero um de _____.

    A E café?

    B _____ um cafezinho.

5 Fill in the bubbles with the correct form of the verb **ter**, plus the word which describes what the people in the pictures are feeling.

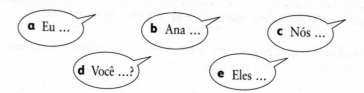

a Eu ...

b Ana ...

c Nós ...

d Você ...?

e Eles ...

6 Look at the various bills from restaurants, and match them to the amounts paid below.

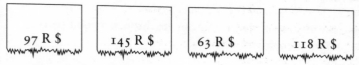

97 R $ 145 R $ 63 R $ 118 R $

- **a** sessenta e três reais
- **b** cento e quarenta e cinco reais
- **c** noventa e sete reais
- **d** cento e dezoito reais

7 Indicate where the following food and drink items would appear on a menu, by ticking the appropriate columns.

		starter	main meal	side dish	dessert	drink
a	sorvete					
b	água					
c	café					
d	sopa					
e	bife					
f	legumes					
g	camarão					
h	farofa					

Testing yourself – do you understand?

Look at the following menu, then the preference of the people dining out with you. Choose a 3-course meal suitable for all concerned.

Laura is a vegetarian and cannot eat sugar.

Marcelo hates fish/seafood but loves to eat white meat. He loves coconuts.

Sérgio is allergic to shrimps and doesn't like starting a meal with soup. He enjoys eating a mixture of meats in a main meal, and loves very sweet desserts.

You can't manage a starter, but can get through a good steak. You prefer ice-cream for afters.

Rita is very traditional, and likes to start her meal with good, hot broth, followed by fish and likes something fresh for dessert.

	Starter	Main Meal	Dessert
Laura			
Marcelo			
Sérgio			
You			
Rita			

Restaurante o Paraná

Cardápio

Entradas

Camarão a Paulista
Creme de aspargos
Lula frita
Canja

Prato Principal

Bife na Brasa
Frango assado
Peixe à minuana
Ovelha na Brasa
Espeto misto
Omelete de queijo
Todos servidos com arroz,
legumes e batatas

Sobremesa

Doce de coco
Pudim de caramelo
Sorvetes e Sorbet
Fruta

9

Vai viajar?
Are you going travelling?

In this unit you will learn
- *How to use public transport*
- *How to ask for change*
- *How to find out departure and arrival times*

Dialogue 1

Sylvia decides to travel northwards to the cities of Salvador and Fortaleza in the **nordeste**. She needs a taxi to get to the coach station. Listen to her conversation at the taxi rank (**o ponto de táxi**).

CD1, TR 10, 00:07

Sylvia	Pode me levar à estação rodoviária, por favor?
Motorista	Posso, sim, sem problema. Vai viajar?
Sylvia	Sim, vou para o nordeste, passar uns dias em Salvador e Fortaleza.
Motorista	Cidades bonitas. Também precisa visitar a cidade de Olinda; é muito histórica e faz parte de nosso patrimônio.
Sylvia	Vou tentar.
Motorista	Aqui estamos.
Sylvia	Quanto é?
Motorista	16 reais. Boa viagem.

pode/posso *can you/I can*
levar *to take*
estação (a) rodoviária *bus station*
sem problema *no problem*
viajar *to travel*
passar *to spend (time), to pass*
precisa *you need*
faz parte de *it's part of*
nosso patrimônio *our heritage*
tentar *to try*
boa viagem *bon voyage*

Dialogue 2

Sylvia goes to the ticket office (**a bilheteria**) to purchase her coach ticket.

Sylvia	A que horas parte o próximo ônibus de luxo para Salvador?
Empregado	Parte às dez e quinze.
Sylvia	Queria um bilhete para este, se faz favor.
Empregado	De ida ou de ida e volta?
Sylvia	Só de ida.
Empregado	Muito bem. Agora, são 68 reais.
Sylvia	Tem troco para uma nota de cem reais?
Empregado	Sim, tenho. Tome.
Sylvia	Obrigada. O ônibus sai de onde?
Empregado	Sai do portão número 22. É por ali à esquerda.

o próximo *the next*
bilhete (o) *ticket*
de ida/de ida e volta *single/return*
tem troco para? *do you have change for?*
uma nota de *a … note*
sai de onde? *where does it leave from?*
o portão número 22 *gate no 22*

Grammar

Pode me levar ...? *Can you take me ...?*

In Unit 1 you learnt the Portuguese words known as personal pronouns for *I, you, he,* etc. used as subjects of verbs. In the dialogue above, you were introduced to another pronoun, this time an object of the verb, i.e. one to whom (or which) the action is done directly. In English these *direct object pronouns* are: *me, you, him, her, us, them.* In Portuguese they are:

me	*me*	**nos**	*us*
te	*you*	**os**	*them, you* (pl.)
o	*him, you, it*	**as**	*them, you* (pl.)
a	*her, you, it*		

In English you may have examples such as *I can see you, you write it quickly, they hit us,* etc. Usually, in standard written Portuguese, these object pronouns are placed after the verb and attached to it by a hyphen (except in certain situations, e.g. negatives or questions). However, the Brazilians tend to place the object pronouns before the verb, whether in a positive or negative statement.

Eu o escrevo	*I write it* **(eu escrevo-o)**
Eles nos batem	*they hit us* **(eles batem-nos)**
Você não me vê	*you do not see me*

Often Brazilians will use the object **te** for *you*, instead of **o/a**, despite these latter being the correct forms corresponding to você. Thus: **Eu te vejo** *I see you*, and not **Eu o/a vejo**. In colloquial Portuguese, Brazilians may quite often say things like **eu vejo você** *I see you*, which is incorrect, or **eu vejo ele** *I see him* (literally *I see he*).

> ## Insight
> It is often the case that pronouns are omitted if there was previous reference to the noun: **Você comprou o livro? Sim, comprei.** *Did you buy the book? Yes I bought (it).*

Nosso _Our_

Nosso is the remaining possessive for you to learn. Here is a reminder of the full table of possessives. Remember to choose the possessive word relating to the object possessed.

	m. sing	_f. sing_	_m. pl._	_f. pl._
eu _I_	meu	minha	meus	minhas
você _you_	seu	sua	seus	suas
ele _he_	o ... dele*	a ... dele	os ... dele	as ... dele
ela _she_	o ... dela*	a ... dela	os ... dela	as ... dela
nós _we_	nosso	nossa	nossos	nossas
vocês _you_	seu	sua	seus	suas
eles/elas _they_	o ... deles /delas*	a ... deles /delas	os ... deles /delas	as ... delas /delas

*If there is no ambiguity, for all forms of _his/her/their_ you can also use **seu, sua,** etc. Don't forget, you will also come across examples of **o meu/a nossa,** etc. For example:

Nosso amigo	_Our friend_
A casa dele	_His house_
João é o meu amigo;	_John is my friend;_
sua casa é grande.	_his house is big._

Insight
24-hour clock

When travelling, be aware of times given using the twenty-four hour clock. Providing you know your numbers up to 59, you should be OK. The actual structure is a simple adding process, as you learnt in Units 5 and 6, joining the two sets of digits by '**e**' (_and_).

Às dez e quinze	_At 10:15_
Às treze e trinta e seis	_At 13:36_
Às vinte e duas e quarenta e cinco	_At 22:45_

Dialogue 3

Having arrived in Salvador, Sylvia needs to get to the centre.

Sylvia	Desculpe, senhor. O que faço para chegar ao centro da cidade?
Sr	Você vai para onde exatamente?
Sylvia	Não sei muito bem. Ao centro.
Sr	Bem, tome o ônibus número 5A, que parte daqui, da frente da estação rodoviária, e sai na praça Vicente, que é bem no centro da cidade.
Sylvia	Obrigada. O senhor conhece um bom hotel aqui?
Sr	Sim, o hotel Beira-mar é muito bom, e não é nada caro.
Sylvia	Onde é este hotel?
Sr	É na Rua Jorge Amado, número 35.
Sylvia	Muito obrigada.
Sr	De nada.

QUICK VOCAB

o que faço para ... *what do I do in order to ...*
exatamente *exactly*
da frente de *from in front of*
é bem ... *it's right ...*
não é nada caro *It's not at all expensive*

Grammar

How do I ...?

In the dialogue, this expression was translated as **o que faço para?** (*what do I do in order to?*). You may also come across:

como se faz para ...?   *how does one ...?*
como posso ...?   *how can I ...?*

Both are followed by verbs in the infinitive.

In front of: prepositions

Prepositions – words of place, location, position – are varied in Portuguese. You met some in Unit 3 which you may like to revise. Here are some more you will find useful when discovering where things are:

em frente (de)	*in front (of)*	**ao lado (de)**	*next to*
detrás/atrás (de)	*behind*	**perto (de)**	*near (to)*
debaixo (de)	*under*	**em cima (de)**	*on top (of)*
dentro (de)	*inside*	**fora (de)**	*outside*
entre	*between*	**contra**	*against*

Don't forget that if you are describing a permanent fixture, e.g. a building, you will use **ser** (*to be*) or **ficar**, but with temporary or moveable items, **estar**. For example:

O mercado é/fica perto do cinema.	*The market is near the cinema.*
Minha casa é ao lado da praça.	*My house is next to the square.*
O livro está em cima da mesa.	*The book is on top of the table.*

Test yourself

pode me levar a ... por favor?	*can you take me to ... please?*
vou passar uns dias em ...	*I'm going to spend a few days in ...*
precisa visitar ...	*you need to visit...*
a que horas parte/chega?	*at what time does it depart/arrive?*
o próximo trem/ônibus (de luxo)	*the next train/coach*
queria um bilhete	*I'd like a ticket*
de ida/de ida e volta	*single/return*
tem troco para uma nota de ...?	*do you have change for a ... note?*
... sai de onde?	*from where does ... leave?*
o que faço para chegar a ...?	*how do I get to ...?*

Insight
Transport in Brazil

Taxis are pretty cheap. You can hail them in the street or wait at a **ponto de taxis**.

O ônibus gets very squashed in town centres, with crowds hanging off the back – wherever they can get hold. You get on at the back of many buses and have to go through a turnstyle. It's awkward if you have much luggage, but cheap.

O ônibus de luxo is for long-distance travel and inter-urban. Cheap. Some are more comfortable than others. There are frequent stops at roadside eating places, the basic equivalent of motorway stops. Also known as *ônibus-leito*, where your seat expands into a bed.

O trem is cheap but very slow. Most longer travel is preferable by coach. Probably the most infamous is the **trem da morte** – the train of death, which crosses the swamplands of the Pantanal into Bolivia.

Practice

1 Insert the correct possessive word in these sentences. You may have to think first about the sentence structure in some of them.
   a Estes são [*my*] _____ sapatos [shoes].
   b Sonia é [*his*] _____ amiga. [careful!]
   c [*our*] _____ casa fica perto do cinema.
   d [*their* f.] _____ irmãs são americanas.
   e Esta é [*your* sing.] _____ chave?

2 Can you do the following?
   a Say can you take me to the town centre?
   b Wish someone a good journey.

c Ask what time the next coach to Rio departs.

d Ask if someone has change for a R$50 note.

e Ask how one gets to the Miraflores Square.

f Ask someone if they know a good restaurant here.

3 Fill in your part of the dialogue at the bus station, and practise it by listening to the recording.

CD1, TR 10, 02:13

You	*(Ask what time the next coach to Fortaleza departs.)*
Empregado	Parte às vinte e uma e dez.
You	*(Say you'd like a return ticket.)*
Empregado	Muito bem. São 78 reais.
You	*(Ask if he has change for a R$100 note.)*
Empregado	Sim, tenho. Tome.
You	*(Ask where the coach leaves from.)*
Empregado	Sai do portão número 11B. É aqui em frente.

4 Match up the Portuguese statements on the left with the corrrect English version on the right.

a Eu te conheço.   **i** They don't hear me.

b Eles não me ouvem.   **ii** We buy them.

c Miguel o escreve devagar. **iii** The teacher punishes us.

d A professora nos castiga. **iv** I know you.

e Nós as compramos.   **v** Miguel writes it slowly.

5 The following dialogue in a taxi has become scrambled. Can you put it in the correct order?

a Sim, vou passar uma semana em Minas.

b Aqui estamos.

c Pode me levar à estação, por favor?

d Região bonita. Precisa visitar a cidade de Ouro Preto.

e Quanto é?

f Posso, sim senhora. Vai viajar?

g Vou tentar.

h 17 reais. Obrigado.

Testing yourself – do you understand?

Look at the travel information below and answer T/F to these statements.

1 Ticket a was issued for travelling by plane.
2 With Ticket b you'll be travelling on a bus.
3 Ticket c is for a one-way journey.

a

```
Empresa Brasileira de
Infra-Estrutura
Aeroportuária


Série E      No. 279853




TARIFA DE EMBARQUE VOO
     DOMÉSTICO    2a
        categoria


Aeroporto: Salvador /
    Data: 23/05/03
```

b

c

```
Empresa Auto Ônibus Silva S/A


Rio ←→ Recife Ida e Volta / Data de emissão: 12/06/03
Preço : R$ 56,85
```

10

Tem um apartamento livre?

Do you have a room free?

In this unit you will learn
- *How to obtain a hotel room*
- *How to make minor complaints*
- *More about Brazilian meals and meal times*

Dialogue 1

Sylvia approaches the Hotel Florestal in Manaus, Amazon, and enters the reception – **a recepção.**

Rececionista	Boa tarde. Pois não?
Sylvia	Boa tarde. Tem um apartamento livre?
Rececionista	Simples, ou duplo?
Sylvia	Simples por favor. Com banheiro.
Rececionista	Todos os apartamentos têm banheiro. Vamos ver. É para quantos dias?
Sylvia	Para cinco dias, até quinta-feira.
Rececionista	Bom, temos o apartamento 222 livre.
Sylvia	Quanto é por noite?
Rececionista	58 reais, incluindo o café da manhã.
Sylvia	Está bem. Onde fica o apartamento?
Rececionista	Fica no segundo andar, com vista para o rio. Quer preencher esta ficha antes de subir?

◉ CD1, TR 11, 00:09

um apartamento livre *a room free*
simples/duplo *single/double*
para quantos dias? *for how many days?*
por noite *per night*
incluindo *including*
café da manhã (o) *breakfast*
com vista para o rio *overlooking the river*
preencher *to fill in*
ficha (a) *form*
antes de subir *before going up*

Once in her room Sylvia studies the hotel information guide (see following page).

tabela de preços (a) *price tariff*
c/café = com café *with breakfast*
quarto (o) *room*
meia pensão (a) *half board*
pensão complete (a) *full board*
duas camas *2 beds (twin)*
por pessoa *per person*
refeições (as) *meals*
servem-se *are served*
borboleta (a) *butterfly*
a partir das ... *from ... onwards*
cama de casal (a) *double bed*

Exercise 1

Can you work out the solutions to the following, based on the hotel opposite?

a Mr and Mrs Johnson would like a twin room, with full board for 2 nights. How much would they pay in total?
b Are they able to have breakfast served in their room?
c If they asked to have dinner at 'seis e meia da tarde', would it be available?

HOTEL FLORESTAL

Tabela de preços:	quarto só	c/café	meia pensão	pensão completa
apartamento simples	R$40	R$58	R$75	R$95
apartamento duplo (duas camas)	R$35	R$53	R$70	R$90
apartamento duplo (cama de casal)	R$32	R$50	R$67	R$87

Preços por pessoa por noite.

Refeições (servem-se no restaurante *Borboleta*)

café da manhã	a partir das 7:30
almoço	das 12:30 até às 14:00
jantar	das 19:00 até às 21:30

Grammar

Antes de ... *Before ... ing*

To say *before (or after) ...ing something,* in Portuguese you use the prepositions **antes de** *before* or **depois de** *after* plus the infinitive. For example:

antes de subir   *before going up*
depois de descer   *after going down*

You can also use other prepositions with infinitives in the same way, such as **em vez de** *instead of*, **sem** *without* and **além de** *as well as*.

Servem-se refeições *Meals are served*

In Unit 2 you met reflexive verbs – verbs where the action was carried out on or by a 'self': **eu me levanto** *I get myself up*. You can also use reflexive verbs to convey a neutral verb subject, in the same way the French use 'on' (one). **Servem-se refeições** means *meals serve themselves*, i.e. *they are served*. This provides an alternative to saying *we serve* (**servimos**). You may also come across such examples as:

vende-se or **se vende** *for sale*   **compra-se** or **se compra** *is bought*
fala-se or **se fala** *is spoken*   **faz-se** or **se faz** *is made*

> ## Insight
> Keep a look-out for further examples, especially on signs and in adverts. When you are in Brazil, take every opportunity to consider the everyday written language around you; it will help you remember points of grammar you have been studying.

Dialogue 2

Sylvia is on her way to look at the grand Opera House in Manaus. At reception she overhears a conversation.

Hóspede (guest)	Queria me queixar de algumas coisas de que não estou muito contente.
Rececionista	Qual é o problema, senhor?
Hóspede	Em primeiro lugar, o ar-condicionado não está funcionando, e com este calor e tantos mosquitos que temos aqui, não aguento ficar no quarto como está agora. Também a torneira da pia não fecha e a água continua pingando toda a noite.

Rececionista	Peço mil desculpas. Vou chamar alguém para vir ver o quarto já já. Está bem?
Hóspede	OK, mas também precisa trocar o travesseiro por que está sujo, e dar uma olhada às persianas que não abrem direitinho.
Rececionista	Muito bem, senhor. O senhor quer ir jantar enquanto organizo tudo?

QUICK VOCAB

queixar-se de *to complain about*
contente *happy*
em primeiro lugar *first of all*
ar-condicionado (o) *air-conditioning*
não está funcionando *isn't working*
mosquitos (os) *mosquitoes*
como está agora *as it is now*
torneira (a) *tap*
pia (a) *basin*
não fecha *doesn't close*
continua pingando *carries on dripping*
peço mil desculpas *I'm very sorry*
alguém *someone*
já já *right away*
travesseiro (o) *pillow*
sujo *dirty*
dar uma olhada *to have a look*
persianas (as) *blinds*
direitinho *properly*
enquanto *whilst*
organizo *I organize*

Exercise 2

Name three things wrong with the guest's room.

1
2
3

Grammar

Making complaints

In a country as huge as Brazil, it is unfortunately inevitable that something will go wrong at some point. Look at the following check-list of useful expressions:

o aquecimento *heating*	
a luz *electricity*	
a água *water*	não funciona/
o ar-condicionado *air conditioning*	não está funcionando
o chuveiro *shower*	*doesn't work/*
a fechadura *lock*	*isn't working*

a toalha *towel*		sujo *dirty*
os copos *glasses*	está/estão *is/are*	partido *broken*
o garfo *fork*		lascado *chipped*
a faca *knife*		
a colher *spoon*		
o prato *plate*		

Remember to make adjectives agree with the noun, e.g.

as toalhas estão sujas *the towels are dirty*

The verb '**faltar**' (*to be lacking, missing*) is used 'back to front'. **Falta um garfo** – *a fork is missing*, **faltam copos** *the glasses are missing/there aren't any glasses*

Remember to complain politely! Use **desculpe** to start with, and expressions such as:

pode vir ver	*can you come and look*
pode ajudar	*can you help*
é capaz de	*are you able to*
é possível	*is it possible*

Test yourself

tem um apartamento livre?	*do you have a room free?*
simples/duplo	*single/double*
com/sem banheiro/café da manhã	*with/without bathroom/breakfast*
para ... dias/pessoas	*for ... days/people*
fica no ... andar	*it's on the ... floor*
queria me queixar de ...	*I'd like to complain about ...*
o/a ... não está funcionando	*the ... isn't working*
falta/m ...	*there's ... missing*
pode dar uma olhada/ajudar/vir?	*can you have a look/help/come?*
peço mil desculpas	*I'm really sorry*

Insight

Apartamento is the term used in Brazil for an *en-suite room*, otherwise **um quarto** (*room only*) is asked for. A **pousada**, unlike in Portugal, is a *B&B*, although some may be quite pricey. Usually breakfast is included in the price of the room, and certainly worth having – normally a selection of ham, cheese, fruit, cakes and bread rolls. There is a good Youth Hostel service in many parts of Brazil (**os albergues de juventude**), and many motels are also worth considering.

Practice

◀) **CD1, TR 11, 01:23**

1 Take part in a dialogue on the recording about booking a room. Follow the pictures below for your prompts.

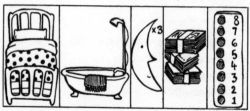

2 Match up the signs with the pictures.

| Se vende | Se fazem | Se compram | Se fala | Se servem |

◆ CD1, TR 11, 02:46

3 Listen to someone booking into a hotel and fill in their details on the **ficha** below.

```
Room type - - - - - - - - - - - - - - - - - - - - - - - - - - - - - - - - - -

With/without bathroom - - - - - - - - - - - - - - - - - - - - - -

No. days - - - - - - - - - - - - - - - - - - - - - - - - - - - - - - - - - - -

Departure day - - - - - - - - - - - - - - - - - - - - - - - - - - - - - -

Room No. - - - - - - - - - - - - - - - - - - - - - - - - - - - - - - - - - -

Price per night - - - - - - - - - - - - - - - - - - - - - - - - - - - - -
```

4 What complaint might you give in each of the following situations? Start with **Desculpe, ...**
   a a dirty fork
   b air conditioning not working
   c dripping tap

d broken plate

e spoon missing

5 Choose an appropriate verb from the box to complete the sentences.

   a Antes de _____ à cidade, vou ver minha amiga.
   b Vá ao seu quarto sem _____ o jantar!
   c Ana vai viajar depois de _____ o trabalho.
   d O senhor quer sentar antes de _____ o filme?
   e Em vez de _____ água, vou tomar um chá.

> ir   terminar   comer   ver   beber

Testing yourself – do you understand?

Look at the information taken as a room booking at the Hotel Ipanema, and answer the questions which follow it.

HOTEL IPANEMA INFORMAÇÃO TURÍSTICA	
Nome *Roberto*	Sobrenome *Silvini*
Endereço *Via Romani, 45, Napoli*	Nacionalidade *Italiano*
Idade *38 anos*	No. telefone *5-867 – 268 – 9961*
Pagamento *Cartão crédito*	Número de crianças, com idades / / /
Tipo de alojamento *Apartamento c/pensão completa*	Quantos quartos? *Um apt. duplo – cama de casal*
Refeições: *Café / jantar*	Quantas noites? *6*
Extra no quarto: *TV / geladeira*	Data da estadia: *Do 5 ao 11 de janeiro*

1 Where is the client from?
2 How is he going to pay the bill?
3 How many rooms does he want?
4 Apart from a TV, what else does he want in the room?
5 What is the client's surname?
6 How old is he?
7 How many children will be coming?
8 Which meals does he want?

11

Que tal esta?
What about this one?

In this unit you will learn

- *How to further discuss likes and dislikes*
- *How to express preference*
- *How to shop for souvenirs*
- *How to buy snacks*

Dialogue 1

Before she leaves Amazônia, Sylvia visits a craft shop to buy some souvenirs.

Sylvia	Bom dia. Estou procurando presentes para minha família. Tem alguma coisa típica do Brasil?
Vendedora	Temos lembranças muito bonitas aqui – típicas da região, e todas feitas a mão. O artesanato aqui é indígeno, feito pelas tribos do Amazonas.
Sylvia	Quanto custa esta bolsa?
Vendedora	Esta é de couro e custa 24 reais. Gosta?
Sylvia	Sim, adoro, mas tem uma menor? É para minha irmã e ela prefere uma bolsa pequena.
Vendedora	Que tal esta? Também é bonita. Ou tem este chaveiro.
	(Contd)

◆ CD2, TR 1, 00:11

Sylvia	Prefiro a bolsa. Agora, que tem para homens?
Vendedora	Temos cachimbos, carteiras, botas, bengalas …
Sylvia	Bom, meu marido detesta fumar, então não vale a pena levar cachimbo. Acho que ele vai ficar encantado com uma bengala.
Vendedora	E para si?
Sylvia	Mm, para mim, bem, eu gosto muito de brincos. Tem?
Vendedora	Temos estes feitos de plantas e de plumas – uma recordação linda desta magnífica parte do mundo.
Sylvia	Tem razão. Então levo os brincos, a bolsa e a bengala. Obrigada.

estou procurando *I'm looking for*
presente (o) *gift*
lembranças (as) *souvenirs*
região (a) *region*
feitas a mão *hand-made*
artesanato (o) *handicrafts*
indígeno *indigenous*
tribo (a) *tribe*
o Amazonas *the Amazon*
que tal esta? *what about this one?*
chaveiro (o) *key-ring*
para homens *for men*
cachimbo (o) *pipe*
carteiras (as) *purses/wallets*
bengalas (as) *walking sticks*
fumar *to smoke*
não vale a pena *it's not worth it*
encantado *very happy*
brincos (os) *earrings*
feitos de plantas/plumas *made of plants/feathers*
recordação (a) *reminder*
esta magnífica parte *this magnificent part of*
do mundo *the world*

Grammar

Likes, dislikes

In Unit 6 you learnt how to use verbs of liking, disliking and preferring, when talking about your favourite leisure activities. In this dialogue you can see how the same verbs are used when referring to objects: **Ela prefere uma bolsa pequena** *she prefers a small bag*. Be careful with the spelling of **odiar** *to hate*: **odeio/ odeia/odiamos/odeiam**; and don't forget **preferir – prefiro/prefere/ preferimos/preferem**.

Para você *For you*

When using the preposition **para** (*for*) with pronouns, you should use the following:

	mim *me*	**nós** *us*
	ele *him/it*	**eles** *them*
para for	**ela** *her/it*	**elas** *them*
	si *himself/herself/yourself/itself*	**si** *themselves/yourselves*
	você *you*	**vocês** *you*

| **Eu gosto de fazer coisas para eles.** | *I like doing things for them.* |
| **Elas fazem tudo para si.** | *They do everything for themselves.* |

These forms of pronouns are also used with other prepositions. Look at these examples:

| **João pensa sempre em mim.** | *John always thinks about me.* |
| **Ela se esquece de nós.** | *She forgets us.* |

Insight

Lembranças do Brasil *Souvenirs from Brazil*

As you travel around Brazil you will come across varied and exquisite souvenirs. Here are a few suggestions for what to buy:

gaucho-style tea and drinking vessel	**chá erva mate (chimarrão) e cuia (cambuca)**
precious stones	**pedras preciosas**
gold	**ouro**
diamond	**diamante**
leather goods	**artigos de couro**
earthenware pottery	**cerâmica de barra**
wall hangings	**tapeçarias**
hammocks	**redes**

I once brought back a **'berimbau'** – a type of musical instrument looking rather like a bow and arrow. The airline shrink-wrapped it and stored it in the hold as it was considered dangerous!

Souvenir expressions

Revise shopping expressions, such as:

posso ver/experimentar
gosto mais deste/daquele
tem outro/menor/maior
tem em + *colour*
de que é feito?

Dialogue 2

Sylvia meets a friend for a quick snack before getting ready to leave for Brasília.

Sylvia	Oi, Paulo. Tudo bem?
Paulo	Tudo, e você?
Sylvia	Ótimo. Esta viagem é muito interessante para mim. Amanhã parto para Brasília.
Paulo	Vai achar Brasília super-diferente – moderna, a sede do governo.
Garçom	Que vão tomar?
Sylvia	Para mim um café com leite e um lanche.
Garçom	De que? Temos hambúrguer, cheesebúrguer-maionese, coxinhas e empadas.
Sylvia	Ai, que difícil! Acho que quero uma empada. Paulo, o que você vai pedir?
Paulo	Para mim, um suco de maracujá, uma coxinha, e um sanduíche de queijo.

QUICK VOCAB

esta viagem *this journey*
um lanche *a snack*
parto para *I leave for*
que difícil! *how difficult!*
vai achar *you'll find*
super-diferente *really different*
a sede do governo *the seat of government*

Snacks and drinks in Brazilian cafés

Bebidas *Drinks*

frio/a	*cold*	**quente**	*hot*
guaraná (o)	*national soft drink*	**chá (o)**	*tea*
vitamina (a)	*milk shake*	**café (o)**	*coffee*
leite (o)	*milk*	**média (a)**	*milky coffee*
suco de fruta (o)	*fruit juice*		
chope (o)	*draught lager*		
laranjada (a)	*orangeade*		

Lanches *Snacks*

bolo (o)	*cake*
sanduíche (o) de – presunto/queijo	*ham/cheese sandwich*
torrada com manteiga (a)	*toast with butter*
coxinha (a)	*chicken 'drumstick'*
empada (a)	*pie*
cheesebúrguer/maionese (o)	*cheeseburger/mayonnaise*

Test yourself

estou procurando presentes para ...	*I'm looking for presents for ...*
tem alguma coisa típica?	*do you have anything typical?*
que tal este/esta?	*what about this?*
que tem para ...?	*what do you have for ...?*
levo ...	*I'll take ...*
para mim, para meu irmão	*for me, for my brother*
o que vai pedir?	*what are you going to have?*
um sanduíche de queijo/presunto	*a cheese/ham sandwich*
quero um lanche	*I want a snack*

Practice

1 Complete the sentences by using the correct form of a verb of liking/disliking, plus the appropriate name for the souvenir in the picture.

   a Ela (odiar) a _____.

   b Eu (não gostar) dos _____.

c Nós (preferir) _____ a
_____.

d Você (gostar) dos _____?

e Eles (adorar) os _____.

2 Choose the correct pronouns out of those given.
  a Este bolo é para **me/mim**.
  b Joana não gosta **deles/dos**.
  c Você pensa **nela/na**?
  d Fazem o trabalho para **se/si**.
  e O livro é para **você/o**.

3 Read each person's snack preferences, then choose what each
would have.
  a Sarah wants a hot drink   **1** cafezinho   **2** média
      without milk
  b Tony is vegetarian   **1** sanduíche de presunto
                                       2 torrada
  c Sally prefers sweet things   **1** bolo   **2** coxinha   **3** empada
  d David wants an alcoholic   **1** suco   **2** chope   **3** chá
      drink
  e Mary hates soft drinks   **1** guaraná   **2** leite
                                       3 laranjada

4 Take part in a dialogue on the recording, where you are buying souvenirs for your family.

You	*(Say I'm looking for presents for my family.)*
Sra	Temos umas coisas bonitas e típicas do Brasil.
You	*(Say do you have a hammock?)*
Sra	Temos estas, que são bonitas.
You	*(Ask how much it is.)*
Sra	Esta custa 156 reais.
You	*(Say what do you have for ladies.)*
Sra	Para senhoras temos tapeçarias, pedras, artigos de couro …
You	*(Say I'm going to take the hammock, and this wall hanging.)*
Sra	Obrigada.

Testing yourself – do you understand?

Mônica is a 'national heroine' in Brazilian cartoon strips. How much of the text below can you understand?

1 In how many countries has Mônica already made her presence felt?
2 When is she going to be launched elsewhere?
3 In how many other countries?
4 In the US marketplace, where will Mônica have to be seen to be attending?
5 In Brazil, what else is the Sousa Production Company launching?
6 What do you think are the words for:
  a little rabbit **b** cartoons **c** classes

Mônica vai às aulas

Com o coelhinho na mão, a personagem Mônica ataca outra vez. Presente timidamente em dezessete países, a partir do ano que vem a heroína dos quadrinhos de Maurício de Sousa vai penetrar com força total em quarenta outros, começando pelos Estados Unidos. Para entrar no mercado americano, Mônica terá de frequentar uma escola. Lá, não se admite faltar às aulas nem nas histórias em quadrinhos. No front interno, a Maurício de Sousa Produções lança o guaraná da Mônica e outros refrigerantes.

12

Por que não vamos ao teatro?
Why don't we go to the theatre?

In this unit you will learn
* *How to plan an evening out*
* *How to get tickets for entertainment*
* *How to make an invitation*
* *More about time*

Dialogue 1

Whilst Sylvia is in Brasília she meets up with an old friend, Luciane. They are trying to decide what to do later that day.

CD2, TR 2, 00:08

Luciane	Que quer fazer mais tarde?
Sylvia	Não me importo. Decida você.
Luciane	Que tal o cinema?
Sylvia	Se quiser. Que filme está passando?
Luciane	Deixe-me ver no jornal. Dê-me aqui. Bom, página 16, aqui está – guia de espetáculos vida noturna. Hmm, no cinema Tivoli está passando 'JFK', no ABC está passando 'Aliens', e no Brasilense 'Wall Street'.
Sylvia	Ai, Lû, você sabe que não gosto nada destes tipos de filmes.

Luciane	Então, fazer o quê?
Sylvia	Por que não vamos ao teatro? Veja o que está passando.
Luciane	Bem, tem uma peça satírica no teatro Marisol – é sobre a política no Brasil de hoje em dia. Parece bem recebida pelo público.
Sylvia	Ótimo. Vamos lá. A que horas começa?
Luciane	Há uma sessão matiné às 3.15 da tarde, e a sessão da noite começa às 7.30. Que horas são agora?
Sylvia	São 2.20. Ainda dá tempo para chegar. Vamos de táxi, é mais rápido. Vamos!

mais tarde *later*
não me importo *I'm not bothered*
decida você *you decide*
se quiser *if you like/want*
filme (o) *film*
deixe-me ver *let me see*
guia (o) *guide*
página (a) *page*
não gosto nada de *I don't like at all*
fazer o quê? *do what?*
veja *see/look!*
peça (a) *play*
satírica *satirical*
sobre *about*
política (a) *politics*
hoje em dia *nowadays*
parece bem recebida *it seems well received*
público (o) *public*
a que horas começa? *what time does it start?*
sessão matiné (a) *matinee*
ainda dá tempo *there's still time*
rápido *quick*
vamos! *let's go*

QUICK VOCAB

Exercise

Can you answer these questions in Portuguese based on the dialogue?

  a Qual é o filme no cinema ABC? _____
  b Os filmes são brasileiros? _____
  c Que tipo de peça há no teatro Marisol? _____
  d Lû e Sylvia vão à sessão da tarde ou da noite? _____
  e Que tipo de transporte elas vão usar? _____

_____

Grammar

Dê-me aqui – *more object pronouns*

In the expression **dê-me** (*give me*), what you are actually saying in Portuguese is *give to me*. In order to say *to me, to you*, etc. you need another set of object pronouns, called indirect object pronouns. They are:

me *to me*	**nos** *to us*
lhe* *to him/her/it/you*	**lhes** *to them/you*

***te** (*to you*) is used more frequently than **lhe**, although often incorrectly.

You use these each time the English has the word *to* in front of the pronoun. You have to be on the look-out, though, because often this is omitted in English. Study this sentence:

Give him the book.

If we break it down, we have:

verb	indirect object (pronoun)	direct object (noun)
give	TO him	the book

In Portuguese this would then be: **dê-lhe o livro**, or colloquially in Brazil: **lhe dê o livro**.

You will also hear **dê o livro para ele**. This is often the case in colloquial speech. In fact, many Brazilians use the word '**dá**' for '*give*', which is normally the command form for the '**tu**-form' of the verb not actually used much there. Nevertheless, you will not go far without hearing: **me dá ...** (*give me...*).

Pronouns galore!

So far you have met quite a variety of these types of words, and as many people find these small expressions confusing, let's compare them all in a table to help you recognize and learn them.

subject	direct object	indirect object	reflexive
eu	me	me	me
você ele ela	o, a (+te)	lhe (+te)	se
nós	nos	nos	nos
vocês eles elas	os, as	lhes	se

Changes following verbs

With direct object pronouns in the third person (**o, a, os, as**), certain spelling changes occur after verbs, which help pronunciation. These changes take place in the following situations:

a Following verb forms ending in -r, -s, and -z

These final letters are omitted, and an -l is added to the beginning of the pronoun. In the case of the omission of final -r, the following written accents are added to the remaining final vowel of the verb.

-ar verbs:	**-á**
-er verbs:	**-ê**
-ir verbs:	**-i** (no accent)

Vou vender meu carro *I'm going to sell my car*
Vou vendê-lo *I'm going to sell it*

b Following verb forms ending in **-m**, **-ão**, and **-õe** (nasal sounds)

The endings are maintained, but an **n** is added before the pronoun to preserve the nasal sound.

Eles fazem o bolo *They make the cake*
Eles fazem-no *They make it*

Remember that in standard Portuguese usage, object pronouns *usually* follow the verb. However, Brazilian usage is more fluid, and in the spoken language particularly, you will find the pronouns before the verb in many instances.

To accent or not to accent?

It can be confusing to come across similar words with the addition, or absence, of written accents, as in the following. This is what they mean:

(o) **que**(?) = *that, which, what(?)*
(o) **quê?** = *what?* (used on its own)
por quê? = *why?* used on its own, or at end of sentence
porque = *because*
por que ...? = *why ...?*

Look at these examples:

Gosto muito de café. Por quê? Porque é muito saboroso.
O que você vai comprar? Um avião. O quê?
Por que não vai ao cinema? Porque é tarde.
O cinema que eu prefiro é perto de minha casa.

Making suggestions

You can use the following expressions:

Que tal ...?	*What about ...?*
Que tal o teatro?	*What about the theatre?*
Que tal a gente* ir ao museu?	*What about us going to the museum?*

*a gente = colloq. *us*

Por que não vai/vamos ...?	*Why don't you/we go ...?*
Que prefere fazer?	*What do you prefer to do?*
Que quer fazer?	*What do you want to do?*
Vamos ...?	*Let's/shall we ...?*

Possible replies might include:

ótimo	*great*	**prefiro/preferia**	*I prefer/would prefer*
está bem	*OK*	**quero/queria**	*I want/would like*
OK	*OK*	**boa ideia**	*good idea*
não estou a fim de ...			
I don't feel like ...			

Describing events

Here are some positive and negative adjectives you may want to use to talk about the cinema, theatre, etc.

É um filme *film*	**romântico** *romantic*
uma peça *play*	**satírico** *satirical*
um concerto *concert*	**cômico** *comical*
uma coleção *collection*	**triste** *sad*
uma exposição *exhibition*	**dramático** *dramatic*
um show *show*	**interessante** *interesting*
	chato *boring*
	fascinante *fascinating*
	crítico *critical*

Starting/finishing times

The rules you learnt for time in Unit 5 apply to the starting and finishing times of events:

A que horas começa?	*What time does it begin?*
Começa às …	*It begins at …*
A que horas termina?	*What time does it finish?*
Termina às …	*It finishes at …*
Há um intervalo {**das … às …** / **de 15 minutos**	*There is an interval* {*from … to …* / *of 15 minutes*

Dialogue 2

♦ CD2, TR 2, 01:49

After the play, Sylvia and Lû decide on the rest of the evening.

Sylvia	Que boa peça! Foi ótima. Só que não entendi tudo.
Lû	Às vezes é difícil – você precisa saber tudo sobre os políticos e a corrupção neste país. Mas gostei.
Sylvia	E agora, Lû. Que fazemos? Voltamos a pé ou apanhamos um táxi?
Lû	Por que não tomamos um copo ali naquele barzinho, e depois vamos jantar naquele restaurante de que você gosta?
Sylvia	Mas preciso me preparar para amanhã – vou viajar por Goiânia.
Lû	Venha, eu te convido, e sou eu quem paga.
Sylvia	Ai, isso não, a gente divide.
Lû	Não, insisto. Você é minha convidada aqui e hóspede neste país. Pago eu.
Sylvia	Está bem. Aceito. E você pode me falar acerca do estado de Goiás.

foi *it was*
só que *only/just that*
não entendi *I didn't understand*
tudo *everything*
políticos (os) *politicians*
corrupção (a) *corruption*
gostei *I enjoyed (it)*
que fazemos *what shall we do?*
tomamos um copo *let's have something to drink*
barzinho (o) *small bar*
preparar *to prepare*
venha *come on!*
eu te convido *I'll treat you*
sou eu quem pago *I'll pay (I'm the one who'll pay)*
isso não *no/oh, no*
a gente divide *we'll split it*
insisto *I insist*
convidada *guest (f) (invited)*
hóspede (o, a) *guest*
pago eu! *I'll pay*
aceito *I accept*
acerca de *about*
estado (o) *state*

Grammar

Talking about the past

In the dialogue you were introduced very briefly to ways of talking about the past in Portuguese.

foi *it was*   **não entendi** *I didn't understand*   **gostei** *I liked*

You will learn the full formations and explanations in Unit 15.

Barzinho *Little bar*

One way of making things smaller, cuter, more affectionate in Portuguese is to add **-zinho** (or **-inho**) to the ending of the word in question. Hence:

o bar → o barzinho	*little bar*
o café → o cafezinho	*little coffee*
o livro → o livrinho	*little book/pamphlet*
o gato → o gatinho	*kitten*
obrigado → obrigadinho	*thanks very much*

Particular means of transport

When specifying a particular vehicle, e.g. a friend's car, or a timetabled bus/train, etc. you use **em** (**no/na**) and the vehicle, and not **de**. For example:

Vou no carro de José.	*I'm going in José's car,* lit. *in the car of José.*
Ele vai no avião da TAM.	*He's going on the TAM plane.*
Vamos no trem das 2.30.	*We're going on the 2.30 train.*

Test yourself

que quer fazer mais tarde?	*what do you want to do later?*
que tal o cinema/o teatro?	*how about the cinema/theatre?*
não me importo	*I don't mind*
se quiser	*if you like/want*
por que não vamos ao museu?	*why don't we go to the museum?*
ainda dá tempo para ...	*there's still time to ...*
há um filme/uma peça/um show	*there's a film/play/show*
eu te convido	*it's my turn to pay for you* *(I invite you)*
sou eu quem pago/pago eu	*I'll pay*
você é meu/minha convidado/a	*you're my guest*

Insight

Brazilians love enjoying themselves, and don't need a lot to make them happy. Even a drink in a bar can proceed into a table-patting, match-box shaking accompaniment of a song, and soon the whole place is alive with movement, rhythm and enjoyment. Larger towns and cities are blessed with museums, cinemas, theatres, nightclubs, galleries and plenty of places to eat, drink and soak up the atmosphere. For the more cultured visitor, there are concerts and literary events as well – just look in the local paper or ask at the **Turismo**.

Insight

If you don't fancy going out (although you'll miss Brazil if you don't), there are always the amazingly dramatic TV soap operas – the **telenovelas**. Brazilians are hooked on them, some watching three, four or five of them daily! And we thought the Aussie soaps were abundant enough!

Practice

1 Can you do the following?
  a Suggest to a friend that you go to the museum.
  b Ask at what time the film starts.
  c Say the concert finishes at 10.30 pm.
  d Say 'What a good exhibition'.
  e Tell John that he is your guest.
  f Say 'Shall we return by bus?'

2 Choose the correct pronouns from those given in the box, to fill the gaps.
  a _____ _____ levanto às sete horas.
  b Dá- _____ o bolo!
  c Não _____ importas?

d _____ vai ao mercado.

e Vou vendê- _____ à minha amiga.

::

          me   ele   eu   te   lo   lhe

::

◆) CD2, TR 2, 03:05

3 Listen to two people discussing how to spend the afternoon,
   and complete the exercise below by ticking the appropriate
   boxes, or filling in the missing information:

a	Marta suggests going to	**i** cinema	**ii** concert
b	What page is the info. on?	**i** 26	**ii** 23
c	What is Rui's preferred activity?	**i** museum	**ii** cinema
d	What is on offer there?	_____	
e	What time?	_____	
f	How will they get there?	**i** bus	**ii** walk

4 Fill in your part of the dialogue, inviting a friend out.

::
Friend	E agora. Que fazemos?
You	(*Say why don't we go and have lunch in that little bar over there?*)
Friend	Mas preciso me preparar para o trabalho.
You	(*Say come along, I invite you and I'll pay.*)
Friend	Isso não.
You	(*Say I insist – you are my guest.*)
Friend	Está bem. Aceito.
You	(*Say let's go.*)
::

5 Fill in the gaps with a *preposition* [*prep.*] (**de/a/em**) or a *means
   of transport*, *location*, or *time*, according to the instructions.
   Don't forget the contracted forms **no, da, à** etc. – see Unit 2.

E.g.   *à*   *cidade*   *de*   🚌   *ônibus*
     Vou [*prep.*] [THE TOWN] [*prep.*]

(a) Sónia vai viajar [*prep.*] [*prep.*] TAM.

(b) Eles vão pegar o [*prep.*] **14:00**

(c) Vamos [*prep.*] ? Não, prefiro ir [*prep.*]

(d) Quer vir [*prep.*] [*prep.*] meu pai?

Testing yourself – do you understand?

Read the three film excerpts that follow to get the gist of each one.

Now answer the following:

a Which film is not American?
b Which film would you choose if you enjoy police stories?
c Which war does film c relate to?
d Is film a comedy or tragedy?
e How many people are killed in film b?
f The adaptation for film c is taken from what source?

a Mulheres à beira de um ataque de nervos

> Este é talvez o filme mais popular do mais consagrado cineasta espanhol: Pedro Almodóvar. Premiado em Berlim com os galardões destinados ao melhor realizador e à melhor atriz (Carmen Maura), o filme é, no fundo, uma grande tragédia, cujas situações levam o espectador a rir até às lágrimas.

b Brigada de Homicidis

O detetive Robert Ross tenta incriminar um perigoso traficante de droga. Mas quando está prestes a deslindar o caso, é-lhe entregue o caso do assassínio de uma velha judia, cujo móbil terá o roubo. Por um lado, o assassínio da velha senhora desperta nele as velhas tradições a que nunca ligou. Por outro, o seu colega é morto, o que obriga Ross a dividir-se pelos dois casos.

Nascido a 4 de julho

c Nascido a 4 de julho de 1946, Ron Kovic oferece-se aos 20 anos como voluntário para o Vietname, desejoso de servir o seu país. Ferido em combate, torna-se paraplégico e herói nacional. Escreve as suas memórias e é esta autobiografia que Oliver Stone (*Platoon, Wall Street, JFK*) – também combatente no Vietname – adapta, num filme que recebe o Oscar de melhor realizador. Para o papel do protagonista, Stone escolheu, contra a opinião de muitos, Tom Cruise, e o jovem ator é na composição da figura de Kovic.

13

É tudo?
Is that everything?

In this unit you will learn
- *How to obtain postal services*
- *How to buy groceries*
- *How to deal with car hire, parking and petrol*

Dialogue 1

Sylvia has bought some postcards (**postais**), and goes to the post office (**correio**) to buy stamps.

Sylvia	Bom dia. Quanto custa enviar um postal para Inglaterra, por favor?
Empregada	2 reais e cinquenta centavos.
Sylvia	E este pacote? Por via aérea?
Empregada	Ponha na balança. Agora, pesa um quilo e cem gramas, então custa 7 reais e noventa centavos.
Sylvia	Bom, então queria seis selos para postais, e quero enviar o pacote também.
Empregada	São 22 reais e noventa centavos no total.
Sylvia	Aqui tem uma nota de cinquenta.

(Contd)

◆ CD2, TR 3, 00:08

Empregada	*(counts change)* Agora dez centavos dá vinte e três, vinte e quatro, vinte e cinco, trinta, e vinte dá cinquenta.
Sylvia	Obrigada. Onde é a caixa?
Empregada	É ali à direita; ponha no lado esquerdo, onde diz 'estrangeiro'.

enviar *to send*
postal(o)/postais *postcard/s*
pacote (o) *parcel*
por via aérea *by air mail*
ponha *put*
balança (a) *scales*

pesa *it weighs*
quilo (o) *kilo*
gramas (os) *grammes*
no total *in all*
caixa (a) *post box*
estrangeiro (o) *abroad*

Dialogue 2

Next Sylvia goes to a local grocery store (**a mercearia** or **minimercado**) to buy some food for her few days away in the countryside.

CD2, TR 3, 01:26

Dono *(owner)*	Bom dia. Pois não?
Sylvia	Bom dia. Queria pão por favor. Tem pãezinhos?
Dono	Aqui. Quantos quer?
Sylvia	Meia dúzia. E um pacote de manteiga.
Dono	Que mais?
Sylvia	Tem presunto?
Dono	Temos este, que é muito bom, ou aquele *(pointing)*, que também é saboroso.
Sylvia	Me dê 250 gramas deste aqui, por favor.
Dono	Mais alguma coisa?
Sylvia	Sim, tem um bom queijo?
Dono	Este queijo é excelente. Quer provar um pedaço deste?
Sylvia	Mmm, que delícia. Me corte meio quilo por favor.
Dono	É tudo?

Sylvia	Só faltam umas garrafas de água, uma de guaraná, que adoro, e estas coisinhas que tenho aqui no carrinho.
Dono	Muito bem. São 36 reais no total. Obrigado e boa viagem.

pãezinhos (os) *bread rolls*
quantos? *how many?*
meia dúzia *half a dozen*
pacote (o) *packet*
excelente *excellent*
pedaço (o) *bit*
é tudo? *is that everything?*
só faltam *they're just missing/needed*
que mais? *what else*
saboroso *tasty*
deste *of this*
mais alguma coisa? *anything else?*
provar *to taste, try*
que delícia *how delicious*
me corte *cut (for) me*
garrafas (as) *bottles*
coisinhas (as) *few things/little things*
carrinho (o) *trolley*

True or false?

Answer **verdadeiro** or **falso** to these statements.

V   F

a Sylvia quer comprar oito pãezinhos.
b O senhor não tem presunto.
c Sylvia prova um queijo antes de comprar.
d Sylvia compra uma garrafa de cerveja.

Grammar

Quantities for shopping

Weights and measures

1 k	um quilo	1 l	um litro
½ k	meio quilo	½ l	meio litro
250 g	250 gramas	250 dl	um quarto de litro
100 g	100 gramas		

Other quantities

um pacote *packet*
um rolo *roll*
uma barra *bar*
uma lata *tin, can*
uma caixa *box*
um tubo *tube*
um frasco *jar*
um saquinho *little bag*

....

Insight
One of this, some of those

These expressions are often lifesavers when you do not know, or cannot remember, the names of items. You can simply point and say:

um/uma *one*
uns/umas *some*
um pouco *a little*

- **deste/desta** *of this* (m/f)
- **destes/destas** *of these*
- **daquele/daquela** *of that* (m/f)
- **daqueles/daquelas** *of those*

And if you don't know whether what you are pointing at is masculine or feminine, say '**um pouco disto**' (*a bit of this* *thing*), or **200 gramas daquilo** (*200 g of that thing*). These are more neutral expressions and very handy.

This here, that there

You have already learnt that **este** (or **esta**) means *this* (*thing here*), and **aquele** (or **aquela**), means *that* (*thing there*). There are also the words **esse, essa, esses, essas,** which refer to the thing nearest the person with whom you are talking.

a esta flor aqui
this flower here

b essa flor aí (que
você tem)
*that flower (you
have there)*

c aquela flor ali
*that flower
over there*

Quanto? *How much?*

Quanto is used as an adjective in expressions such as **quantos quer?** (e.g. **quantos pãezinhos**). If you were buying bottles, you would be asked **quantas?** (**garrafas**). Used as a question about cost (**quanto é?**, **quanto custa/m?**, **quanto vale?**) it doesn't change form.

Groceries

The following check list may be useful

os ovos *eggs*
o queijo *cheese*
o mel *honey*
a farinha *flour*
o molho *sauce*
a manteiga *butter*

os biscoitos *biscuits*
os cereais *cereals*
o azeite *olive oil*
o açúcar *sugar*
a massa *pasta*
o pão *bread*

Test yourself

Here is a summary of shopping expressions

Quanto custa?	*How much does it cost?*
Tem?	*Do you have?*
Quanto/a/os/as quer?	*How much/many do you want?*
Que mais?	*What else?*
Me dê/corte (Dê-me) ...	*Give/cut me ...*
Mais alguma coisa?	*Anything else?*
É tudo?	*Is that all?*
Pois não?	*Can I help you?*
São ... no total	*That's ... in all.*
Este, esse, aquele	*this, that, that*

Insight

Post offices usually open from 9 till 6 during the week, although some close for lunch. Postage is expensive in general, as is faxing. The queues are enough to try the patience of a saint, but in larger branches you can now buy stamps at the philatelic desk. You can recognize the Post Office by the ECT sign – **Empresa de Correios e Telégrafos**.

Shops also open at the above times, with the smaller ones closing for lunch (between 11.30 am and 2 pm). On Saturdays shops tend to close at lunchtimes, apart from the larger shopping centres and supermarkets.

Practice

1 Fill in your part of this dialogue in a post office.

You	(*Say good afternoon; how much does it cost to send this parcel to Germany, please?*)
Empregada	Ponha na balança. Agora, dois quilos, então são 13 reais.

You	(*Say right, I'd like to send the parcel, and I would also like 10 stamps.*)
Empregada	Para a Alemanha também?
You	(*Say no, 3 for Spain and 7 for England.*)
Empregada	São 35 reais e setenta centavos.
You	(*Say thank you; where is the post box?*)
Empregada	É ali, à esquerda.

◀)) **CD2, TR 3, 03.52**

2 Look at Miguel's shopping list below, and then listen to his conversation at the minimercado. Tick off everything he buys, put a cross by what is not available, and write down in English the extra item he buys.

½ dúzia de ovos

açúcar

2 pacotes biscoitos

frasco de mel

presunto —
250 gramas

1½ litros cerveja

8 pãezinhos

Extra item = _____

3 Fill in the gaps using the appropriate form of **este**, **esse** or **aquele**.

   a _____ postal aqui é para minha amiga.

   b Qual manteiga? _____ que você tem aí.

   c _____ senhores ali são italianos.

d _____ pãezinhos aqui são muito bons.

e _____ balas que você tem são deliciosas.

4 Grocery bingo. Here is your Bingo card, containing five items of grocery. Listen to the voice on the recording, who will call out various items, and cross off those on your card when you hear them. When you've heard all five, shout Bingo! If you have done so correctly, you should hear the voice congratulate you (**parabéns**).

◄) **CD2, TR 3, 03:50**

Dialogue 3

Sylvia goes to a car-hire agency.

Sylvia	Boa tarde. Eu posso alugar um carro aqui?
Empregado	Claro. Tem todos os documentos necessários?
Sylvia	Aqui, tome.
Empregado	Bom, estão todos em ordem. Agora, é para quantos dias?
Sylvia	Para quatro, começando de hoje. Tem algo econômico, mas ao mesmo tempo confortável? Quero ver um pouco da região.

◄) CD2, TR 3, 04:26

Empregado	Temos um Ford, que custa 53 reais por dia, mais 6 por quilômetro. O preço inclui o seguro.
Sylvia	Ótimo!
Empregado	Agora, é só assinar aqui e aqui, e pronto. Não se esqueça de trazer o carro de volta com o tanque cheio.

QUICK VOCAB

alugar to hire, rent
necessários necessary
em ordem in order
começando beginning
econômico reasonable
ao mesmo tempo at the same time

inclui includes
seguro (o) insurance
não se esqueça don't forget
de volta back
o tanque the tank
cheio full (filled)

Dialogue 4

Whilst she is looking at a map, Sylvia is approached by a policeman (**um policial**).

Policial	Boa tarde. Sabe que é proibido estacionar aqui?
Sylvia	Ah, boa tarde, senhor policial. Ainda bem que está aqui. Parece que estou perdida. O que faço para chegar em Goiânia?
Policial	Goiânia é? Bom, o melhor é virar aqui para a esquerda, tomar aquela estrada, e continuar até ao próximo cruzamento. Depois vai ver os sinais.

◉ CD2, TR 3, 05:30

QV

proibido prohibited
estacionar to park
ainda bem thank goodness
o melhor é the best thing to do is

estrada (a) main road
cruzamento (o) crossroads
sinais (os) traffic signs
perdida lost

Dialogue 5

Later Sylvia stops for petrol.

CD2, TR 3, 06:25

Sylvia	Boa tarde. Ponha 15 litros por favor.
Empregado	De normal, sem chumbo, gasóleo ou de álcool?
Sylvia	Creio que é sem chumbo. É carro alugado.
Empregado	Ah sim; olhe, aqui diz sem chumbo. Então 15 litros. É tudo?
Sylvia	É possível verificar a água e o óleo para mim?
Empregado	Claro. Um momento só. Está tudo OK.
Sylvia	Obrigada.

normal *ordinary petrol/gasoline* (also called just **gasolina** or **combustível**)

gasóleo (o) *diesel* (also called just 'diesel')

sem chumbo *unleaded* (also referred to as '**gasolina comum**')

álcool (o) *alcohol/ethanol* (used in Brazil)

alugado *hired*

olhe *look*

aqui diz *here it says*

verificar *to check*

óleo (o) *oil*

Grammar

Por *for*, **per**, *through*

The preposition **por** *for* is used in expressions with prices, e.g. **reais por dia** *reais per day*. **Por** contracts into **pelo, pela, pelos** and **pelas** when combined with the article, e.g. **vou pela cidade** = *I'm going through (by) the town*.

Verbs as adjectives

Estou perdida/carro alugado, are examples of verbs used as adjectives, what is called the 'past participle'. This is the part in English such as 'seen, broken, parked, opened', etc. In Portuguese, it is formed in the following way:

	remove infinitive ending	add past participle ending	past participle
falar to speak	**-ar**	**-ado**	**falado** spoken
comer to eat	**-er**	**-ido**	**comido** eaten
partir to depart/ leave/break	**-ir**	**-ido**	**partido** departed/ left/broken

Be careful with irregular verbs. Here are some examples:

ver → visto   vir → vindo
fazer → feito   abrir → aberto
escrever → escrito   pagar → pago

Rules of adjectives then apply. For example:

A casa é feita de madeira.   *The house is made of wood.*
As janelas estão partidas.   *The windows are broken.*

You will come across past participles again later, in use as part of a past tense in Portuguese. In the meantime, see how many you can spot in adverts and leaflets.

O melhor é ... *The best thing to do is ...*

This construction can be used with a variety of adjectives as well as with **melhor** (*best*).

O importante é ...   *The important thing is ...*
O pior é ...   *The worst thing is ...*
O triste é ...   *The sad thing is ...*

Insight

Petrol: sugar cane alcohol (ethanol) is the normal fuel, although diesel is also common. Many roads are terrible, some not more than dirt tracks. Insurance in Brazil may not give you full cover, so do be aware of what you are signing for.

_____

Practice

5 Now see if you can do the following:
   a Ask if you can rent a car here.
   b Say it's for 8 days, starting today.
   c Ask what you do to get to Rio.
   d Say 'I seem to be lost'.
   e Say 'Put in 12 litres of alcohol, please'.
   f Ask 'Can you check the water for me?'

6 Choose an appropriate past participle for each sentence from the box and make any necessary alterations to it to use it as an adjective.
   a O banco está _____.
   b Todas as janelas estão _____.
   c Os sapatos são _____ de couro.
   d A conta já está _____.
   e A carta está _____, senhor Mendes.

```
    aberto    pago    feito    fechado    escrito
```

◀》 **CD2, TR 3, 07:23**

7 Listen to someone at a petrol station and indicate on the grid the services they require.

Petrol – tick which type	How much?	Check water/oil	Price
Alcohol/Unleaded/Diesel			

8 Estou perdido ... Fill in the gaps in this dialogue: replace the English words by Portuguese ones.

Policial   (*Good morning*) _____ _____ . É (*prohibited*) _____ estacionar aqui nesta (*town square*) _____ .

Sra.   Desculpe. Acho que estou (*lost*) _____ . O que faço para chegar no (*Rio*) _____ ?

Policial   Bom, o melhor é virar aqui para a (*right*) _____ , seguir até aos (*signs*) _____ , e depois tomar a (*2nd*) _____ à (*left*) _____ , e continuar naquela (*main road*) _____ .

Testing yourself – do you understand?

Can you link up the road signs with their corresponding instructions?

a		**i**	área escolar
b		**ii**	aeroporto
c		**iii**	vento lateral
d		**iv**	cuidado, animais
e		**v**	semáforo à frente
f		**vi**	siga em frente
g		**vii**	vire à direita
h		**viii**	proibido virar à esquerda

i		**ix**	proibido trânsito de bicicletas
j		**x**	siga em frente ou à esquerda
k		**xi**	velocidade máxima permitida
l		**xii**	pedestre ande pela esquerda

14

Está livre amanhã de tarde?
Are you free tomorrow afternoon?

In this unit you will learn
- *How to make plans for the future*
- *How to make arrangements to meet people*
- *How to deal with a telephone call*
- *The months of the year*

Dialogue 1

Sylvia overhears two people discussing their weekend plans whilst she is in a café in Campinas.

Moço *(Boy)*	Que vai fazer sábado de manhã, Teresa?
Moça *(Girl)*	Gostaria de fazer aquela viagem para o Pantanal, já que temos férias neste momento. Quer vir comigo?
Moço	Eu quero, sim. Ouvi dizer que é uma viagem fantástica, a gente viaja no trem da morte, há de ser super-legal.
Moça	Não posso esperar – sempre quis ir. Sabe que a gente pode ver animais – há jacaré e tudo. Vamos até a Bolívia e depois voltamos. Leva mais ou menos uma semana para ir e voltar.

(Contd)

◆ CD2, TR 4, 00:09

Moço	Ótimo. Olhe, eu aos sábados, costumo ir ao mercado bem cedo com minha mãe, mas estou livre a partir das oito e meia. Onde nos vamos encontrar?
Moça	Na rodoviária. Temos que ir primeiro a 'Sampa' para apanhar o trem. Eu estarei lá às nove horas. Tá?
Moço	Tá bem. A gente se vê no sábado. Tchau.
Moça	Tchau. E não se esqueça da máquina fotográfica, tá?

QUICK VOCAB

gostaria de *I would like to*
o Pantanal *swamp area near Bolivia*
já que *seeing as*
férias (as) *holidays*
neste momento *at the moment*
ouvi dizer que *I heard that*
a gente = nós *we*
viaja *travel*
há de ser *it's bound to be/got to be*
super-legal *brilliant, cool*
esperar *to wait*
sempre quis ir *I've always wanted to go*
animais (os) *animals*
jacaré (o) *alligator*
leva *it takes*
costumo *I usually*
bem cedo *really early*
a partir das *from*
encontrar *to meet*
temos que ir *we have to go*
'Sampa' *São Paulo*
estarei *I shall be*
tá = está? *OK*
a gente se vê *we'll see each other*
máquina fotográfica (a) *camera*

Dialogue 2

Back in her hotel, Sylvia has a call from a university aquaintance.

CD2, TR 4, 01:43

Sylvia	Alô?
Nelson	Alô, Sylvia?
Sylvia	Sim, quem fala?
Nelson	Daqui fala Nelson Gusmão, da Unicamp.
Sylvia	Oi, Nelson, tudo bem?
Nelson	Eu estou muito bem. E você?
Sylvia	Tudo azul. Como sabia meu número?
Nelson	Foi o José que me disse. Então, como vai sua grande 'tour' do Brasil?
Sylvia	Estou adorando. Estou fazendo boas amizades e desfrutando do tempo para explorar o país.
Nelson	Bom, você esta livre amanhã de tarde?
Sylvia	Estou, sim. Tenho que fazer um trabalho até ao meio-dia, mas depois estou livre. Por quê?
Nelson	Por que não vamos jogar tênis?
Sylvia	Está bem. A que horas nos encontramos?
Nelson	Às 2.30. Passo pelo hotel para te pegar. OK?
Sylvia	OK. Até amanhã.
Nelson	Tchau. Até amanhã.

alô *hello* (on phone)
daqui fala *this is* (from here speaks)
Unicamp *University in Campinas*
tudo azul *everything just fine*
tempo (o) *the time*
explorar *to explore*
sabia *you knew*
disse *told/said*
amizades (as) *friendships*
desfrutando *taking advantage (of)*
passo *I'll pass*
pelo hotel *by the hotel*

QUICK VOCAB

Grammar

Future plans: *ir* + verbs

The easiest and most common way of talking about future actions is to use the verb **ir** *to go* plus the infinitive of any verb. We do the same in English – *I'm going to visit Italy next summer./We're going to buy a car next week*.

Remind yourself of the formation of **ir** from Unit 3.

Vou visitar minha tia na semana que vem.	*I'm going to visit my aunt next week.*
Jaime vai comprar um livro amanhã.	*James is going to buy a book tomorrow.*
Vamos ganhar na loteria no sábado.	*We're going to win the lottery on Saturday.*

Future plans: future tense

You can also use the future tense to discuss your future actions, although in practice it is used less in spoken Portuguese. It can be used to emphasize particularly important actions. It is formed in the following way:

To the inifinitive of any verb add: -ei   -emos
                                       -á   -ão

e.g. **comprarei**   *I shall buy*
      falarão   *they/you* (pl.) *will talk*

However, there are three exceptions where the spelling of the verb changes slightly:

fazer = **far** + endings
trazer = **trar** + endings
dizer = **dir** + endings

All other verbs follow the regular pattern – a welcome relief to all learners! In Dialogue 1, the girl said **estarei lá** – *I shall be there*. She could also have said **vou estar lá**, and even just **estou lá**. In colloquial Portuguese, it is common to substitute the present tense for the future.

e.g. **Compro um carro amanhã.**   *I'll buy a car tomorrow.*
   Te vejo no domingo.   *See you on Sunday.*

Future plans: future times

You will need some time phrases to express your future actions.

amanhã	*tomorrow*
depois de amanhã	*the day after tomorrow*
a semana/o mês/o ano que vem	*next week/month/year*
o/a próximo/a semana, mês, ano	*next week/month/year*
domingo/no sábado, etc.	*Sunday/on Saturday, etc.*

Gostaria *I'd like*

Gostaria is an example of a verb in what is termed the 'conditional' form. In English, we use the word *would* in conditionals. If you think that conditional actually means there is a 'condition' imposed on the action, it may help you to understand these structures. For example, *I would buy a car* (but I don't have the money). *If I had the money* is the condition. With the example of the verb *to like*, the condition may be seen in terms of *I would like to ... if that's OK/ if I may*. Conditionals can lead into a complex part of Portuguese verb usage; however the actual formation is as straightforward as that of the future tense.

Infinitive +   -ia   -íamos
            -ia   -iam

(**Fazer** becomes **faria**, **trazer** becomes **traria**, and **dizer** becomes **diria**.)

Eu compraria um carro.	*I would buy a car.*
Maria falaria com ele.	*Maria would speak with him.*

Start by using **gostaria**, as it gives you scope to build up confidence using this form of verb. **Gostaria de ver um filme** (*I'd like to see a film*); **você gostaria de visitar o lago?** (*would you like to visit the lake?*).

Obligation

In Portuguese there are various ways to express obligation or *having to do something*. The most commonly used in the spoken language is **ter que** or **ter de**, as in Sylvia's **tenho que fazer um trabalho** ... In English we would say *I've got to* ... Stronger obligation is expressed through the verb **dever** *to have to/must*.

Devo terminar este trabalho antes de sair.	*I must finish this work before going out.*

And in expressions such as:

Eles devem estar perdidos.	*They must be lost.*

There is also the use of the verb **haver** *to have*, plus **de**, which conveys even stronger duty, something which is really bound to happen.

hei de	**hemos de**
há de	**hão de**

For example:

Hei de ganhar na loteria.	*I've just got to win the lottery.*
Há de ser bom.	*It's bound to be good.*

A partir de ... From ...

When you want to say 'from [a certain point] onwards' you use **a partir de** plus a point in time. This can be with the time: **a partir das duas horas** *from 2 o'clock*, or time phrases: **a partir de domingo** *from Sunday*; **a partir do mês que vem** *from next month*, etc.

The gerund: -ing

In Unit 6 you met this formation: **-ando/-endo/-indo**. Sylvia uses a few examples to talk about what she is currently involved in doing: **Estou adorando ..., fazendo ..., desfrutando ...**

With the verb **estar** in the present tense, this structure conveys an action currently taking place. For example:

Eles estão falando.	*They are talking (now).*
Agora estamos dormindo.	*Now we are sleeping.*
Eu estou aprendendo português.	*I am (currently) learning Portuguese.*

Insight

The **pantanal** is a great swampland area bordering the central-west part of Brazil and into Bolivia. The train crosses the middle of it and offers hardy travellers a marvellous panorama of its wildlife – alligators, birds, insects and big cats abound.

The **trem da morte**, or *train of death*, is the subject of many a traveller's tale – you need to watch your belongings, and be wary of people offering you food or drinks.

Insight

Telephone calling – in Rio, particularly, the telephone booths are called **orelhão** *big ear*, because of their design. The number 6 in phone numbers is referred to as **meia** (*half*) – from half a dozen.

Practice

1 Now see if you can do the following:
   a Ask Paul what he's going to do on Wednesday afternoon.
   b Say you'll be there at 10.30.

   c Suggest to your friend that you go swimming.
   d Ask someone what time you'll be meeting.
   e Say you're free from 4.15 onwards.
   f Answer the phone and ask who's calling.

◀) **CD2, TR 4, 02:56**

2 Listen to this telephone conversation between two friends and
    answer the questions below.
    a Who is calling?
    b From where?
    c When does he want to see his friend?
    d What will Paulo be doing?
    e What does Paulo's friend suggest?
    f What time will he pick Paulo up?
    g Where?

3 Make sentences by choosing words from each box, and
    forming the correct part of the future tense. A variety of
    answers may be correct. You will find samples in the Key.

	Time	Person	Action	End
A	amanhã	Cristina	visitar	um bolo
B	o mês que vem	eles	comprar	na loteria
C	no domingo	eu	escrever	Alemanha
D	o próximo ano	a Sra Lopes	ganhar	uma carta
E	depois de amanhã	nós	fazer	um carro

4 Decide what is currently going on in each picture, and write it
    down, forming the correct parts of **estar** and the gerund.
    a Eles [*estar*] _____.
    b A Sra [*estar*] _____.
    c Nós [*estar*] _____.
    d Eu [*estar*] _____.
    e Elas [*estar*] _____.

Dialogue 3

After their tennis game, Sylvia and Nelson chat over drinks.

◆ CD2, TR 4, 03:45

Nelson	Que outras cidades vai visitar?
Sylvia	Bom, só me faltam seis semanas aqui, e quero visitar o sul.
Nelson	Tem que visitar Rio Grande do Sul – a região dos gaúchos e as grandes fazendas. No sul também há bastante indústria.
Sylvia	Sim, gostaria muito de ver Curitiba e também as cataratas de Iguaçu.
Nelson	Vai adorar. Nesta época não tem tantos turistas – os meses piores são durante nosso verão – dezembro, janeiro e fevereiro.
Sylvia	Ótimo. Então sem dúvida visitarei Iguaçu – são as mesmas cataratas que aparecem no filme 'A Missão' acerca dos jesuítas portugueses e suas atividades com os índios aqui.
Nelson	Bom filme. Então, Sylvia, um brinde para o resto da sua viagem. Tchin tchin, e boa viagem.
Sylvia	Saúde, e obrigada.

gaúchos (os) *cowboys/ranchers*
fazendas (as) *ranches/farms*
indústria (a) *industry*
cataratas (as) *waterfalls*
época (a) *season, time*
tantos *so many*
turistas (os) *tourists*
os meses piores *the worst months*
durante *during*
verão (o) *summer*
dezembro *December*
janeiro *January*
fevereiro *February*
sem dúvida *without doubt*
as mesmas *the same*
'A Missão' *The Mission*
jesuítas (os) *Jesuits*
índios (os) *Indians*
brinde (o) *a toast*
o resto *the rest*
tchin tchin *cheers*
saúde *cheers*

Grammar

outro, tanto, mesmo

All of these words change their endings depending on the nouns to which they are referring.

outro	**outra**	**outros**	**outras**	*(an) other/s*
tanto	**tanta**	**tantos**	**tantas**	*so much/many*
mesmo	**mesma**	**mesmos**	**mesmas**	*same*

Tanto on its own can also be used with verbs, to give more information about the action, e.g. **ela fala tanto** – *she talks so* *much.* **Mesmo** can also mean *self:* **Ela mesma vai comprar a casa.** *She herself is going to buy the house.*

Os meses *The months*

◀) **CD2, TR 4, 05:10**

janeiro *January*
fevereiro *February*
março *March*
abril *April*
maio *May*
junho *June*
julho *July*
agosto *August*
setembro *September*
outubro *October*
novembro *November*
dezembro *December*

They are now written throughout the Portuguese-speaking world with a lower-case initial letter.

As estações do ano *The seasons*

o verão *summer*
o inverno *winter*
o outono *autumn*
o primavera *spring*

Insight

Remember that Brazil's summer coincides with winter in the northern hemisphere. December to February can be tremendously hot.

Celebratory expressions

tchin tchin/saúde *cheers*
parabéns *congratulations*
boa viagem *bon voyage*
feliz aniversário *happy birthday*
boa sorte *good luck*
feliz Natal *Happy Christmas*
feliz Ano Novo *Happy New Year*
as melhoras *get well*
boas férias *have a good holiday*
feliz Páscoa *happy Easter*

Test yourself

que vai fazer amanhã?	*what are you doing tomorrow?*
está livre amanhã/sábado?	*are you free tomorrow/Saturday?*
gostaria de ver/visitar ...	*I'd like to see/visit ...*
leva uma hora/um mês	*it takes an hour/month*
estou livre a partir de ...	*I'm free from ...*
alô/quem fala?/daqui fala ...	*hello/who's speaking?/it's ... here*
a que horas nos encontramos?	*at what time shall we meet?*
estou viajando/trabalhando	*I'm travelling/working*
saúde/boa viagem	*cheers/bon voyage*
verão/outono/inverno/primavera	*summer/autumn/winter/spring*

Practice

5 Are these statements, based on Dialogue 3, **verdadeiro** or **falso**?

T   F

  a Sylvia still has 7 weeks left in Brazil.
  b Rio Grande do Sul is a region of farms and industry.

c At the moment there are not many tourists about.
d The worst months are in the spring.
e Sylvia wants to visit a Jesuit Mission.
f Nelson toasts the rest of Sylvia's journey.

6 Look at the following situations and what people are saying. They have become mixed up. Can you decide which expression belongs with which picture?

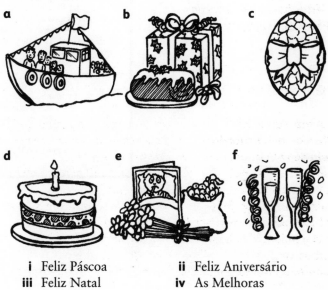

a   b   c

d   e   f

i	Feliz Páscoa	ii	Feliz Aniversário
iii	Feliz Natal	iv	As Melhoras
v	Parabéns	vi	ßoa Viagem

Testing yourself – do you understand?

Your friend has sent you a cutting from a paper about a place she would like to visit with you. Look at the piece and insert the correct words from the box to fill the gaps. Then answer the questions below.

```
flores   festas   Estados   Unidos
      novembro   ano   cores
```

1 What kind of activity is this (music/sport/nature)?
2 What can you see there?
3 What is new this year?
4 When was the event originally set up?

FLORES

Roselândia apresenta festas na primavera

da Redação

Acontecem até o próximo dia 17 de _____, na Roselândia (km 33 da rodovia Raposo Tavares), as _____ da Primavera e das Rosas.

Realizados desde 1954, os eventos mostram novidades em rosas, _____ e plantas ornamentais provenientes da Europa e dos _____ _____ que a Roselândia introduz no Brasil.

Neste _____, além dos jardins com novas variedades de rosas, a novidade são as petúnias, com 15 _____ diferentes.

Informações pelo tel. (011) 7924-0122. (SC)

15

Como foi a viagem?
How was the journey?

In this unit you will learn
- *How to talk in the past*
- *How to discuss a visit you have made*
- *How to describe actions*

Dialogue 1

Sylvia overhears some people talking about their holiday.

Sr	Então, gostou da viagem? Visitou a catedral?
Sra	Adorei. A catedral de lá é tão bonita e típica da arquitetura portuguesa. O nordeste é uma mistura interessante do africano com o europeu – a cultura, a música, e a religião.
Sr	E as pessoas também – pele negra ao lado da branca, olhos pretos, azuis e verdes, cabelos escuros e claros – realmente é o que eles chamam uma miscelânia de culturas.
Sra	Ficamos uma semana na Bahia, uns dias em Salvador e outros em Fortaleza. Assistimos a uma exibição de capoeira na praia, e falamos com os pescadores com suas jangadas.
Sr	Comeram a comida de lá?
Sra	Meu marido provou muitos pratos – vatapá por exemplo, mas eu achei um pouco picante.
Sr	Então, valeu a pena?
Sra	Sem dúvida! Esperamos voltar o ano que vem.

🔊 CD2, TR 5, 00:09

gostou? *did you enjoy?*
visitou? *did you visit?*
adorei *I loved*
tão *so*
arquitetura (a) *architecture*
mistura (a) *mixture*
africano *African*
europeu *European*
cultura (a) *culture*
religião (a) *religion*
pessoas (as) *people*
pele negra (a) *dark skin*
olhos (os) *eyes*
cabelos (os) *hair*
sem dúvida *really, without doubt*
o que eles chamam *what they call*
ficamos *we stayed*
assistimos a *we watched*
capoeira (a) *acrobatic dance*
falamos *we spoke*
pescadores (os) *fishermen*
jangadas (as) *Northeast boats*
comeram? *did you (pl.) eat?*
comida (a) *food*
provou *tasted*
pratos (os) *dishes*
achei *I found/thought*
picante *spicy*
valeu a pena? *was it worth it?*
esperamos *we hope*
vatapá (o) *shrimp dish*

Exercise

Complete these statements with the correct ending:

1 The lady visited **a** the north. **b** the south. **c** the northeast.
2 In Bahia they stayed **a** a week. **b** a few days. **c** two days.
3 She thought the food was **a** too bitter. **b** too spicy. **c** too bland.

Grammar

The past

You have already met one or two expressions where the verb was in the past. To describe an action which was a one-off event, finished, complete, we use what is called the *simple past* (referred to in Portuguese terms as the preterite). In the dialogue, there were various examples, such as:

visitou *you visited*   **ficamos** *we stayed*   **comeram** *you ate*

Let's look at how the simple past of the regular **-ar/-er/-ir** verbs is formed.

	remove infinitive ending	add preterite endings		preterite	
falar *to speak*	-ar	-ei	-amos	falei	falamos
		-ou	-aram	falou	falaram
comer *to eat*	-er	-i	-emos	comi	comemos
		-eu	-eram	comeu	comeram
partir *to depart/* *leave/break*	-ir	-i	-imos	parti	partimos
		-iu	-iram	partiu	partiram

Ela falou comigo.	*She spoke with me.*
Comemos muito.	*We ate a lot.*
Partiram às nove horas.	*They* (you pl.) *left at nine o'clock.*

In Portuguese this tense also translates as *have, has done*. So **falei com ela** can be *I spoke to her*, or *I've spoken to her*.

Insight

Can you spot ending patterns, like you did with the present tense? Notice e.g. **-amos/-emos/-imos**. Note that the Brazilian forms in the *we* person are the same in the present and the

(Contd)

past tenses. You may have to deduce what time zone an
event took place in by looking carefully at the context, and
searching for clues, such as 'yesterday', 'last night', etc.

Past questions

Did you notice the man's questions – **gostou?/visitou?/comeram?** –
simply used the past part of the verb, with no equivalent of the
English *did*. So the questions actually say *you liked (enjoyed) …?/
you visited …?/you ate …?*

O africano/o europeu

You have learnt that **o** + *adjective* is used to convey *the … thing*,
e.g. **o importante**. The examples in our dialogue here are very
similar:

o africano – *that which is African* (the African)
o europeu – *that which is European* (the European)

Dialogue 2

Back in her hotel, Sylvia chats to the receptionist.

CD2, TR 5, 01:27

Rececionista	Quando voltou de Porto Alegre?
Sylvia	Voltei ontem à noite. Apanhei o ônibus das 17 horas e cheguei aqui às 9:30.
Rececionista	Gostou da visita?
Sylvia	Fiquei encantada. Visitamos uma fazenda, andamos a cavalo e comemos com os gaúchos.
Rececionista	Comeu churrasco?
Sylvia	Sim, e bebemos um chimarrão, que é o chá típico da região.
Rececionista	No inverno daqui, até os estudantes bebem este chá nas aulas por causa do frio daqui.
Sylvia	Que interessante. Bom. Tem algum recado para mim?

Rececionista	Deixe ver. Ah sim, o senhor Ferreira acaba de telefonar. Disse que não é urgente.
Sylvia	Está bem, obrigada.

ontem à noite *last night*
fiquei *I became/was*
aulas (as) *lessons*
por causa de *because of*
recado (o) *message*
acaba de *has just*
urgente *urgent*

___

Dialogue 3

Sylvia returns José's telephone call and tells him about her journeys to the north and south of Brazil.

CD2, TR 5, 02:28

Sylvia	Alô, José?
José	Alô, Sylvia, tudo bem? Acabo de ligar para aí.
Sylvia	Eu sei. Me deram o recado agora.
José	Então, como foi a viagem pelo norte?
Sylvia	Foi ótima. Vi tantas coisas interessantes.
José	Foi a Manaus?
Sylvia	Fui, vi o teatro, dei uma voltinha pelo rio – fiz muitas coisas.
José	Foi à fazenda aí?
Sylvia	Sim, acabo de voltar. Os gaúchos são fascinantes – a maneira de viver, a cultura e o Fandango.
José	Dançou também?
Sylvia	Não me atrevi – eles dançam tão rapidamente, eu fiquei sentada.
José	Quando volta para cá?
Sylvia	Bom, amanhã vou para Curitiba, depois visitarei uma amiga num cafezal. Daqui a duas semanas estarei de volta em São Paulo.
José	Ligue para mim antes de partir.
Sylvia	Tchau.

acabo de ligar *I've just rung*
deram *they gave*
vi *I saw*
fui *I went*
dei uma voltinha *I made a little trip*
maneira (a) *way*
viver *to live/living*
Fandango (o) *Fandango dance*
dançou? *did you dance?*
não me atrevi *I didn't dare*
dançam tão rapidamente *they dance so quickly*
sentada *sat down/seated*
cafezal (o) *coffee plantation*
ligue para mim *ring me*

Grammar

Past tense: awkward spellings

Some verbs alter their spellings in the past tense, to maintain certain sounds (hard or soft letters). In the dialogues you had: **cheguei** from **chegar**. Other similar examples are:

jogar – joguei   ficar – fiquei
pagar – paguei   explicar – expliquei
                        tocar – toquei *I played/touched*
                        indicar – indiquei

These changes happen in the first person singular only.

Other verbs also make changes in their spelling. Try to learn them as you come across them, and check in a grammar book for the patterns to learn.

Irregular preterite tense verbs

dar	dizer	fazer	estar	ir	poder	pôr
dei	disse	fiz	estive	fui	pude	pus
deu	disse	fez	esteve	foi	pôde	pôs
demos	dissemos	fizemos	estivemos	fomos	pudemos	pusemos
deram	disseram	fizeram	estiveram	foram	puderam	puseram

saber	sair	ser	ter	trazer	ver	vir
soube	saí	fui	tive	trouxe	vi	vim
soube	saiu	foi	teve	trouxe	viu	veio
soubemos	saímos	fomos	tivemos	trouxemos	vimos	viemos
souberam	saíram	foram	tiveram	trouxeram	viram	vieram

Acabar de *To have just done*

This handy expression is easy to learn, and very useful. You use the present tense of the verb **acabar** (*to finish*), plus **de** plus a verb in the infinitive. For example:

Sr Ferreira acaba de telefonar.   *Mr Ferreira has just telephoned.*
Eu acabo de chegar.   *I've just arrived.*

Aí *There (where you are)*

It is slightly confusing knowing when to use the various words for *here* and *there*.

aqui, cá *here*   **aí** *there*   **ali, lá** *there*
(where I am/we are)   (where you are)   (where neither of us are)

These also correspond to the demonstratives you learnt in Unit 13:

este *this here*   **esse** *that near you*   **aquele** *that over there*

So if you are talking to someone on the phone, you must use **aí** if you want to say e.g. *is it warm there?* – **está quente aí?** If you say **está quente lá?**, you are referring to somewhere distant from your listener.

Slow, slow, quick, quick, slow

Adverbs give us more information about a verb. They answer the question *how?* For example:

They dance. How do they dance? Quickly.

In English many adverbs end in *-ly*.

Eles dançam. Como dançam? Rapidamente.

In Portuguese many adverbs end in **-mente**.

To form an adverb, take the feminine form of an adjective and add **-mente**. If there is no separate feminine form, add **-mente** to the standard form. For example:

rápido → rápida → rapida**mente**
fácil → facil**mente**

There are some irregular adverbs, including:

mal *badly*   **bem** *well*   **devagar** *slowly*   **cedo** *early*

Test yourself

gostou de ...?	*did you like (enjoy) ...?*
visitou a catedral/a praia?	*did you visit the cathedral/beach?*
como foi a viagem?	*how was the trip?*
foi ótimo/maravilhoso/péssimo	*it was great/brilliant/awful*
voltei/apanhei/comi	*I returned/caught/ate*
tem algum recado para mim?	*do you have any messages for me?*
... acaba de telefonar/ligar	*... has just phoned*

daqui a duas semanas	*in two weeks' time*
falam rapidamente	*they speak quickly*
ligue para mim	*give me a ring/call*

Practice

1 Can you do the following?
  a Ask your friend if she visited the museum.
  b Say 'We stayed two weeks in Italy.'
  c Ask José and Sônia when they returned from New York.
  d Ask the receptionist if he has a message for you.
  e Say 'I've just arrived in the hotel.'
  f Say 'The Italians speak so quickly.'

2 Complete the sentences with the correct form of the past tense of the verb in brackets.
  a Ontem eu [*comer*] muito.
  b No ano passado eles [*comprar*] uma casa.
  c Nós [*partir*] à meia-noite.
  d Vocês [*gostar*] da festa?
  e Marcelo [*escrever*] um postal para sua mãe.

3 Choose the correct verb in each sentence.
  a Ela viu/veio João no mercado.
  b Eu fui/fiz um belo jantar.
  c Nós pudemos/pusemos os pratos na mesa.
  d Eles foram/fizeram ao cinema.
  e Você trouxe/teve boa sorte.

4 Complete your part of the dialogue about a visit.

Ricardo	Quando voltou do Rio?
You	(*Say I returned yesterday afternoon. I arrived here at 3.25.*)
Ricardo	Gostou da visita?

(Contd)

You	(Say yes, a lot. I walked on Copacabana beach, visited Sugar Loaf Mountain – Pão de Açúcar – and I saw the shanty towns – **as favelas**.)
Ricardo	Gostou da comida também?
You	(Say yes, I ate **feijoada** and tried the firewater and lime drink.)

5 Form the correct past tense and choose an adverb from the box to go with the pictures overleaf.

> rapidamente   devagar   bem   cedo   mal

    a Eles [*lavantar-se*] _____.
    b Ela [*correr*] _____.
    c Elas [*cantar*] _____.
    d Nós [*falar*] _____.
    e Eu [*tocar piano*] _____.

6 Listen to the dialogue, and fill in the gaps with the words you hear.

CD2, TR 5, 03:52

José	Então, como foi a viagem para _____?
Sylvia	Foi ótima. Vi tantas coisas interessantes.
José	Foi a Londres?
Sylvia	Fui. Fui ao _____, vi o Big Ben, _____ o _____ – fiz muitas coisas.
José	Foi à _____ também?
Sylvia	Sim, acabo de voltar. Os _____ são _____ – a maneira de viver, a cultura e a _____.
José	Dançou também?
Sylvia	Não me atrevi – eles dançam tão rapidamente, eu fiquei sentada.
José	Quando volta para cá?
Sylvia	Bom, amanhã vou para _____, depois visitarei uma amiga. Daqui a _____ estarei de volta em _____.
José	Ligue para mim antes de partir. Tchau.
Sylvia	Tchau.

Testing yourself – do you understand?

Read Teresa's letter and see if you can answer the questions on it.

Minas, 10 de julho de 20 ..

Oi, Cecília, tudo bem?

Acabo de voltar das férias que passei nos Estados Unidos. Foi super-legal. Fiquei com meus tios, que moram na Califórnia. O tempo estava super-quente e gostei imensamente.

Fomos visitar muitos lugares interessantes, e vi as casas enormes dos atores de Hollywood. Passei em frente da casa de Michael Jackson – parece um castelo! Um dia viajamos até Disneyworld, onde passamos muitas horas divertindo-nos. Nunca vi tantas pessoas na vida! Provei a comida de lá – é tudo comida-rápida, tipo hambúrguer e batatas, não é nada saudável. Comprei uma recordação para ti, acho que vai adorar.

Ouvi muita música americana, e na última noite fui a uma discoteca, que legal! A única coisa que realmente detestei foi a falta de guaraná!

Eu te digo mais no sábado, ligue para mim antes de vir,

tchau,

Teresa

1 Onde foi de férias?
2 Como estava o tempo?
3 Viu a casa de quem?
4 Que pensa da comida?
5 Onde foi na última noite?
6 Que detestou mais?
7 Quando vai ver Cecília?

16

Quanto custaram?
How much did they cost?

In this unit you will learn
- *How to talk about what you have bought*
- *How to identify your own property*
- *More about the past*

Dialogue 1

Sylvia listens to some people discussing what they have just bought.

Carlos	Que quadros mais lindos! Onde os comprou?
Isabel	Comprei-os numa lojinha no fim daquela rua ali. A senhora foi super-simpática comigo. Ela me deu um desconto porque comprei dois. Gosta, Paulo?
Paulo	Gosto. São paisagens típicas do sul. Quanto custaram?
Isabel	Não muito. Só 35 reais cada. Uma pechincha, não acham?
Carlos	Realmente!
Isabel	E você, Carlos, comprou alguma coisa?
Carlos	Nós fomos até à feira 'hippy'. Nunca vi tantas coisas bonitas. Que difícil escolher!
Isabel	E daí – que decidiu?
Carlos	Vi estas pedras preciosas, que adorei, e depois compramos esta caixinha de madeira.

(Contd)

◉ CD2, TR 6, 09:09

Isabel	Que bonitinha! Quanto custou? Foi cara?
Paulo	Não, só 13 reais.
Isabel	Puxa! Eu preciso ir lá já. Onde é que fica esta feira?

QUICK VOCAB

que quadros mais lindos! *what beautiful pictures!*
lojinha (a) *small shop*
no fim *at the end*
simpática *kind/nice*
paisagens (as) *landscapes*
quanto custaram? *how much did they cost?*
cada *each (one)*
pechincha (a) *a bargain*
feira 'hippy' (a) *hippy/craft fair*
nunca vi *I've never seen*
escolher *to choose*
e daí? *and so?*
que decidiu? *what did you decide?*
caixinha (a) *small box*
foi cara? *was it expensive?*
puxa! *crikey/wow!*

Exercise

Can you answer the following in Portuguese?

a Que comprou Isabel? _____
b Onde foram os dois senhores? _____
c O que Carlos adorou? _____

_____

Grammar

Exclamations

It's nice to be able to inject exclamations into your dialogues, where relevant, as this makes your Portuguese much more authentic. Portuguese is a very expressive language, and the Brazilians especially love using it in a vibrant and sometimes vociferous way!

These few expressions will suffice for now to get you started:

Que + noun + adjective: **Que vestido lindo!** *What a nice dress!*
And, using **mais**: **Que vestido mais lindo!** *What a gorgeous dress!*
(lit. *what dress most lovely*)

Que coisa mais linda!	*What a lovely/gorgeous thing – isn't it gorgeous! (very common)*
Que legal!	*Cool/wicked/brilliant!*
Ótimo!	*Great/cool/wicked/fantastic*
Puxa!/Puxa vida!	*Gosh!/wow!*
Nossa!/Nossa Senhora	*'Our Lady'/crikey/good God*
E daí?	*And so/And then/And?/So what?*
Opa!/ Oba!	*Whay-hey/yo/ wow/hey*
Que bagunça!	*What a mess!*

Insight

Cada is a handy word meaning *each* or *every*. It never changes form, so you could have:

cada semana = todas as semanas *every week*
cada dia = todos os dias *every day*
cada um/uma custou *each one cost*

Dialogue 2

A lady approaches the table.

CD2, TR 6, 01:22

Márcia	Desculpem, mas acho que a senhora pegou meus óculos de sol. Deixei-os no balcão daquela loja de artesanato ali em cima há meia hora.
	(Contd)

Regina	O quê? Acho que a senhora está enganada. Estes óculos são meus.
Márcia	Mas são óculos especiais porque não vejo muito bem. Olhe, aqui tem a marca Medioc.
Regina	Onde? Ah, sim agora que eu vejo – tem razão. Peço desculpa. Foi sem querer. Então, onde estão os meus?
Ricardo	Aqui, na sua cesta. Que bagunceira!
Regina	Tem toda razão – Desculpe tá?
Márcia	Não importa. Bom dia.

QUICK VOCAB

desculpem *excuse me (to more than one person)*
pegou *you took*
balcão (o) *counter*
há meia hora *half an hour ago*
enganada *mistaken*
são meus *they're mine*
especiais *special*
marca (a) *make, brand*
foi sem querer *I didn't mean to*
cesta (a) *basket*
que bagunceira! *what a mess-pot!*

Grammar

Há + *time*

You can use **há** + a time phrase to mean *ago*, e.g.

há meia hora	*half an hour ago*
há duas semanas	*two weeks ago*
há muito tempo	*a long time ago*

Identifying your belongings

In previous units you have practised the possessive adjectives *my*, *your*, *his*, *our*, etc. Remind yourself of them if you cannot remember them. To identify or claim your property, or that of someone else, you use the same set of possessive words plus the verb **ser**:

estes óculos são meus   *these glasses are mine*
esta casa é nossa   *this house is ours*

You can answer the question **de quem é ...?** *Whose is ...?*, simply by saying:

é ⎫   ⎧ **meu/sua/nossos**, etc.
são ⎭   ⎨ **de Maria**
             ⎩ **dele/dela**, etc.

Insight

Many towns in Brazil have a weekly crafts fair, often referred to as the **feira hippy**. Here you can find a variety of hand-made products, leather goods, jewellery, the beautiful semi-precious and precious stones for which Brazil is renowned, pictures – watercolour (**aquarela**) and oil (**óleo**) – and wax items (**de cera**). Also, there are usually stalls selling food: often you will find **baianas** – the typical women from Bahia (**o nordeste**), dressed in flouncy white clothes – selling the kind of spicy food you would eat in Bahia. The **feira hippy** is a great place to buy presents, and a wonderful place to spend some time drifting around.

Test yourself

que ... mais lindo(s)!   *what beautiful ...!*
onde comprou?   *where did you buy (them/it)?*
quanto custou/custaram?   *how much did it/they cost?*

que difícil escolher!	*how difficult it is to choose!*
puxa!/que legal!	*crikey!/cool!*
acho que está enganado/a	*I think you're mistaken*
tem razão	*you're right*
foi sem querer	*it wasn't on purpose*
há uma hora/algum tempo	*an hour/some time ago*
é meu/minha, são meus/minhas	*it's/they're mine*

Practice

1 Replace **cada** with an appropriate form of **todo** (o/a/os/as), and change the verb forms where this becomes necessary.

   a Ela vai ao mercado [cada semana] _____.

   b Nós gostamos de viajar [cada ano] _____.

   c [cada um dos] _____ livros (custa) _____ R$10.

   d Maria trabalha muito [cada dia] _____.

   e [cada pessoa] _____ (ganha) _____ um presente.

   f Gosto de [cada mês] _____ do ano.

2 Fill in your part of this dialogue about an item you have bought.

Marco	Que vestido mais lindo. Onde o comprou?
You	*(Say I bought it at the hippy-fair in the square.)*
Marco	Quanto custou?
You	*(Say not a lot. Only 42 reais. Do you like it?)*
Marco	Gosto. Foi uma pechincha.
You	*(Ask him, 'did you buy anything?')*
Marco	Comprei este livro numa pequena livraria.
You	*(Say what a most interesting book.)*

3 Complete the sentences with demonstratives (**este** etc.) and possessives according to the pictures and instructions.

a

Este _____ é _____. [*ours*]

b

_____ _____ são _____. [*mine*]

c

_____ _____ é _____ _____. [*of José*]

d

_____ _____ é _____. [yours, of *você*]

e

_____ _____ são _____. [theirs, of *eles*]

4 Listen to four people talking about when they did various activities, and fill in the table below.

◀) **CD2, TR 6, 02:21**

Speaker	Did what?	How long ago?
1		
2		
3		
4		

Testing yourself – do you understand?

Read the following dialogue and/or listen to it on the recording, then answer the questions on it.

◀) CD2, TR 6, 02:54

> **Sra** Desculpe, mas acho que o senhor pegou meu guarda-chuva. Deixei-o no restaurante Mineiro na praça há vinte minutos.
>
> **Sr** O quê? Acho que a senhora está enganada. Este guarda-chuva é meu.
>
> **Sra** Mas é um guarda-chuva especial. Olhe, aqui tem o nome da minha companhia – Empresa Tecnical Limitada.
>
> **Sr** Onde? Ah, sim, agora que eu vejo – tem razão. Peço desculpa. Foi sem querer. Então, onde está o meu?
>
> **Sra** Ali, ao lado da porta daquela loja.
>
> **Sr** Você tem toda razão – Desculpe tá?
>
> **Sra** Não importa. Bom dia.

1 What has he picked up by mistake?
2 Where was it left?
3 When?
4 How is it recognized?
5 Where is the other one?

17

Era tudo tão diferente
It was all so different

In this unit you will learn
- *How to talk about something you saw earlier*
- *How to identify a stranger*
- *How to recall how a place used to be*

Dialogue 1

Sylvia pops back to a shop to buy a skirt she had seen in the window, but finds the display has changed.

Empregada	Bom dia, pois não?
Sylvia	Havia uma saia na vitrine de que gostei muito, mas já não está mais lá.
Empregada	Como era a saia?
Sylvia	Era azul com flores pequenas.
Empregada	E onde estava exatamente?
Sylvia	Estava à esquerda da vitrine, bem na frente.
Empregada	E era de algodão ou de lã?
Sylvia	De algodão. Era muito bonita. Acho que custava 56 reais.
Empregada	Ah, sim, agora estou me lembrando. Só tinha aquela e mais duas daquele modelo, e vendemos as três hoje de manhã.

(Contd)

Sylvia	Ai, que pena!
Empregada	Quer ver as outras saias que temos?
Sylvia	Não, obrigada. Só queria aquela.
Empregada	Está bem. Talvez haja mais na semana que vem.
Sylvia	Está bem.

havia *there was*
vitrine (a) *shop window*
já não está mais lá *it's no longer there*
era *it was*
flores (as) *flowers*
estava *it was*
bem na frente *right in front*
custava *it cost*

estou me lembrando
 I'm remembering
tinha *there was*
modelo (o) *style*
vendemos *we sold*
que pena! *what a pity*
queria *I wanted*
talvez haja *perhaps there will be*

Grammar

Há … havia *There is/are … there was/were …*

Havia is the past equivalent of **há**. Remember you can use **há** to mean *there is/are*. Therefore, **havia** can mean *there was/were*. You may also come across the word **houve**, also meaning *there was/were*, but used to describe one-off happenings, such as:

houve um acidente	*there was an accident*
houve um barulho enorme	*there was a huge noise*
havia muitas pessoas na rua	*there were many people in the street*

Brazilians also use parts of **ter** for the same purpose, e.g. **teve um acidente/teve um barulho/tinha muitas pessoas.**

The past, part 2

In Unit 15 you learnt how to use the simple past (preterite) to describe actions in the past which had been completed. In the dialogue here you are introduced to another past tense, called the *imperfect*. Try to remember it as *imperfect* because usually there is no perfect ending to it – it's more open-ended than the previous past tense. It describes an action which was continuous in the past, going on for some time. Look at the examples from the dialogue:

Como era? (from **ser**)	*What was it like? (all the time)*
Onde estava? (**estar**)	*Where was it? (all the time it was in the window)*
Custava	*It cost (all the time it had a price)*
Só queria esta	*I only wanted this one (all the time)*

Compare these with verbs in the simple past:

Como foi o filme?	*What was the film like? (as a whole)*
Ele me custou	*It cost me (one-off payment)*

It may help to look at the following 'time-line'.

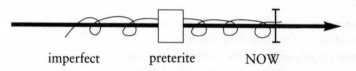

imperfect	preterite	NOW

The imperfect is a continuous line in the past, with often no clear beginning or ending (this can continue right up to the present time – *I wanted it and I still do*). The preterite is safely enclosed in a solid, complete box – it's finished. Often the preterite will interrupt an imperfect one, such as:

I was having a bath WHEN		*the phone rang.*
(continuous)	(sudden point)	(preterite)

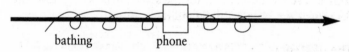

bathing	phone

Formation

	remove infinitive ending	add imperfect endings		imperfect	
falar to speak	-ar	-ava	-ávamos	falava	falávamos
		-ava	-avam	falava	falavam
comer to eat	-er	-ia	-íamos	comia	comíamos
		-ia	-iam	comia	comiam
partir to depart/ leave/break	-ir	-ia	-íamos	partia	partiámos
		-ia	-iam	partia	partiam

e.g. **Ela falava comigo.** *She was speaking to me.*

You will also come across the common construction **ela estava falando …** See next unit.

Watch out for these irregular verbs:

pôr *to put*	punha, punha, púnhamos, punham
ser *to be*	era, era, éramos, eram
ter *to have*	tinha, tinha, tínhamos, tinham
vir *to come*	vinha, vinha, vínhamos, vinham

Insight

When you have got an idea about using the two past tenses you have learnt, try to spot them in the written language: children's books are a good source of material for this.

Dialogue 2

CD2, TR 7 01:28

Sylvia has had a visitor at her hotel.

Rececionista	Senhora Peters, havia um senhor aqui que a procurava.
Sylvia	Um senhor? Como era?

Rececionista	Era bastante alto, tinha cabelo preto, e um bigode, e estava vestido de terno cinzento.
Sylvia	Como ele se chamava?
Rececionista	Não sei. Não disse o nome.
Sylvia	Mas o que ele queria?
Rececionista	Também não sei. Só disse que voltava mais tarde.
Sylvia	Ele tinha que idade?
Rececionista	Bom, provavelmente 50 e tantos anos.
Sylvia	Ah, já sei quem era. É o pai duma amiga minha que tem um cafezal aqui. Vou ficar uns dias com a família dela. Bom, vou subir.

procurava *was looking for*
como era? *what was he like?*
bastante *quite*
alto *tall*
bigode (o) *moustache*
vestido *dressed*
terno (o) *suit*
como ele se chamava? *What was he called?*
voltava *he was returning/would return*
idade (a) *age*
provavelmente *probably*
50 e tantos anos *50-odd*
pai (o) *father*
uma amiga minha *a friend of mine*
subir *to go up (stairs)*

QUICK VOCAB

Grammar

People descriptions

Notice which verbs were used in the descriptions.

era from **ser** – for permanent characteristics
tinha from **ter** – possession, hair/eyes/beards, etc., age

estava from estar – temporary characteristics/states, what they are wearing

If you want to describe people in detail, you will need:

height	alto *tall* médio *medium* baixo *small, short*
build	grande *large* gordo *fat* forte *strong* pequeno *small* magro *thin*
eyes	os olhos + colour
hair	o cabelo + colour comprido *long* curto *short* liso *straight*
extras	bigode *moustache* barba *beard* **óculos** *glasses* careca *bald*
clothes	revise Unit 7

Uma amiga minha *A friend of mine*

To express *a ... of mine/of yours*, etc. place the noun first, followed by the appropriate possessive. For example:

uns sapatos seus	*some shoes of yours/his*, etc.
uma amiga nossa	*a friend of ours*

Dialogue 3

Sr Mendes shows Sylvia round the coffee plantation, and explains how things used to be.

Sr Mendes	Tudo é muito diferente agora. Antigamente havia menos tecnologia, não havia tantas máquinas, e mais pessoas trabalhavam por aqui.
Sylvia	Mas, não é mais fácil hoje em dia?
Sr Mendes	Isso, sim, mas também é um pouco mais impessoal. Antes a gente falava muito, comíamos juntos, íamos a bailes nas outras fazendas, e ajudávamos uns aos outros. Hoje existe muito mais competição.
Sylvia	E a cidade, mudou também?

Sr Mendes	Mudou, sim. Todos os dias íamos ao centro, tomar um cafezinho, falar com os amigos, e depois jogávamos cartas e a vida passava na valsa. Hoje é tudo movimento, rápido, dinheiro.
Sylvia	Mas pelo menos tem uma bela fazenda.
Sr Mendes	Sim, casa, família, boa comida e um estilo de vida que não tínhamos antes – sim, tudo tem recompensa. Vamos ver os processos lá dentro?
Sylvia	Vamos, e depois um bom cafezinho!

antigamente *before, in the past*
tecnologia (a) *technology*
máquinas (as) *machines*
trabalhavam *they used to work*
impessoal *impersonal*
íamos *we used to go*
bailes (os) *dances*
existe *there exists*
competição (a) *competition*
jogávamos *we used to play*
movimento (o) *rush*
dinheiro (o) *money*
pelo menos *at least*
bela *lovely*
tínhamos *we had, used to have*
recompensa (a) *reward*
processos (os) *processes*
mudou *it has changed*
a vida passava na valsa *life went with the flow*
ajudávamos uns aos outros *we used to help one another*
estilo de vida (o) *lifestyle*

Grammar

The imperfect – the way we used to be

Another function of the imperfect tense is to describe how things 'used to be' or things you 'used to do'. You can introduce statements with expressions like:

antes/antigamente/no passado — *before/in the past*
quando era jovem/éramos jovens — *when I/you/he was young/we were young*
quando morávamos em … — *when we used to live in …*

Look at these examples:

Quando João morava na Índia, bebia chá todos os dias.
When John lived (used to live) in India, he drank (used to drink) tea every day.

Antes de me casar, eu trabalhava num banco.
Before I married, I worked (used to work) in a bank.

Test yourself

havia ...	*there was/were ...*
já não mais está (lá)	*it's no longer (there)*
como era?	*what was it like?*
onde estava?	*where was it?*
só queria este/esta	*I only wanted this one*
o que (ele) queria?	*what did (he) want?*
era alto/gordo/forte	*he was tall/fat/strong (large)*
50 e tantos anos	*50-odd/50-ish*
antigamente dançávamos	*we used to dance in the past*
um amigo meu/seu/nosso	*a friend of mine/yours/ours*

Practice

1 Now can you do the following?
   a Say there was a blouse I liked in the shop window.
   b Say it was on the right of the display.
   c Say she was short, with long hair and blue eyes.
   d Say he was probably 40 or so years old.
   e Ask is it not more interesting nowadays?
   f Say we used to swim every day.

2 Decide in each case whether the verb should be in the imperfect or the preterite (simple past) tense.
   a Ontem eu fui/ia à cidade para comprar um selo.
   b Quando era/foi jovem, Carlos fumava.

   c Nós jantamos/jantávamos quando o telefone tocou.
   d Antigamente eles comiam/comeram muito mal.
   e Na semana passada ela veio/vinha à minha casa.
   f Onde estava/esteve você quando eu te telefonei?

◄) **CD2, TR 7, 04:12**

3 Listen to descriptions of people, and decide which articles of clothing go on each body.

4 Form the correct part of the imperfect tense for the verbs, and link them to the second part of the sentence.

Quando éramos jovens ...
   a ir _____   **i** mais energia.
   b brincar _____   **ii** aos bailes.
   c ter _____   **iii** férias com nossos pais.
   d estudar _____   **iv** no campo.
   e passar _____   **v** todos os dias.

5 Complete your part in this dialogue in a shop.

You	*(Say there was a shirt in the shop window, but it's not there now.)*
Emp.	Como era?
You	*(Say it was black and was made of wool.)*
Emp.	E onde estava exatamente?
You	*(Say it was on the left of the display, behind the trousers.)*
Emp.	Ah sim, lamento, mas vendemos aquela ontem. Quer ver os outros modelos que temos?
You	*(Say no thanks. I only wanted that one.)*
Emp.	Está bem. Adeus.

6 Link up the following descriptions with the correct pictures.

i   ii   iii   iv

a João é alto e forte. Tem cabelo curto e liso e um bigode. Está vestido de terno e chapéu.

b Sabrina é de estatura média e magra. Tem cabelo comprido. Usa óculos.

c Lúcia é baixa e um pouco gorda. O cabelo dela é liso e curto, e ela está vestida de saia e blusa.

d Maurício é alto e magro. É careca.

18

O que você tem?

What's the matter?

In this unit you will learn
- *How to describe illness and ailments*
- *How to deal with the chemist and doctor*
- *How to cope with an accident*
- *How to say goodbye*

Dialogue 1

Sylvia has returned to the Ferreira's house in São Paulo, but has woken up not feeling very well.

◀ CD2, TR 8, 00:09

Sylvia	Marli, não me sinto nada bem.
Marli	O que você tem?
Sylvia	Estou com dor de barriga e tenho uma dor de cabeça.
Marli	Parece muito pálida. Vou chamar nosso médico. Fique aí na cama até ele chegar.
	[40 minutos mais tarde]
Médico	Onde dói, senhora Peters?
Sylvia	A barriga e a cabeça. Os olhos também me doem.
Médico	Que comeu ontem?
Sylvia	Ontem à noite saímos para um restaurante e eu comi um arroz com mariscos.

Médico	E em geral tem algum problema quando come peixe?
Sylvia	Geralmente não. É grave?
Médico	Não se preocupe, senhora Peters. Creio que é só uma pequena alergia. Fique onde está, na cama, até sábado, e tome este medicamento.

não me sinto nada bem *I don't feel at all well*
o que você tem? *what's the matter?*
me dói/doem ... *my ... hurts/hurt*
barriga (a) *belly*
dor (a) *pain*
cabeça (a) *head*
pálida *pale*
médico (o) *doctor*
fique *stay*
cama (a) *bed*
até ele chegar *until he arrives*
saímos *we went out*
arroz com mariscos(o) *seafood risotto*
grave *serious*
não se preocupe *don't worry*
creio que *I think/believe that*
alergia (a) *allergy/reaction*
medicamento (o) *medication*

True or false?

Mark these statements **verdadeiro** or **falso**.

                                                   V   **F**

  a Sylvia has a sore stomach.
  b Her teeth also hurt.
  c Last night she ate steak and rice.

Grammar

1 Feeling ill

To express ailments, you can use the verb **doer** *to hurt* in the following way:

indirect object pronoun + **doer** + part/s of body

| **me** | **dói** | **a cabeça** = *my head hurts* |
| **lhe** | **doem** | **os olhos** = *his/her/your eyes hurt* |

What you are doing is saying that **x** gives pain to you/him, etc.

You can also use:
    ter uma dor de ... *(to have a pain of ...)*
    ter uma dor em (no, na, nos, nas) ... *(to have a pain in/on ...)*
    estar com dor de/no, na, nos, nas ... *(to be with pain in/on the ...)*

These are most common in Brazil.

| **Tenho uma dor de cabeça.** | *I have a headache.* |
| **Ele tem uma dor nos olhos.** | *He has sore eyes.* |

Other useful expressions:

uma enxaqueca	*a migraine*
ter gripe	*to have a cold*
ter insolação	*to have sunstroke*
cortar	*to cut*
magoar	*to hurt*
bater	*to hit*
sentir-se enjoado/a	*to feel nauseous*
vomitar/passar mal	*to vomit/to be sick*

O corpo *The body*

You cannot describe where your pain is adequately without knowing the parts of the body, although you can just point and say '**me dói aqui**' *it hurts me here*. Here is a body and head for you to study.

Dialogue 2

When she goes to the chemist (**a farmácia**) to pick up Sylvia's medicine, Marli overhears another customer.

Farmacêutico	Bom dia. Diga por favor.
Cliente	Tem alguma coisa para dor de garganta?
Farmacêutico	Sim, temos estas pastilhas que são excelentes, ou este xarope.
Cliente	Levo as pastilhas.
Farmacêutico	É só?
Cliente	Não, o que tem para queimaduras de sol?
Farmacêutico	Hmm, este creme é bom. É só 2 reais e 40 centavos.
	(Contd)

CD2, TR 8, 01:22

Cliente	Bom, levo dois frascos.
Farmacêutico	Então, são 7 reais e 80 centavos.
Cliente	Também preciso de alguma coisa para meus lábios – estão muito secos.
Farmacêutico	Tem isto, que é novo –é um batom transparente que protege o lábio antes e depois do sol.
Cliente	Muito bem. Vou experimentar.
Farmacêutico	Agora são 8 reais e 45 centavos. Adeus e espero que melhore!

Grammar

Medicines

Here are a few useful items you may need to purchase at the chemist's:

aspirina (a) *aspirin*
um band-aid *a plaster*
um colírio *an eyewash*
antihistamínico(o) *antihistamine*

Subjunctive verbs

The expression **Espero que melhore** *I hope that you get well (better)* introduces us to another area of verbs in Portuguese, which is extremely complex, and which causes the most concern to learners as they progress a little further. We are only going to touch lightly upon it as an introduction.

So far, you have learnt some different tenses of verbs, to help you talk in various time zones. Now we are going to look at something called the *subjunctive* mood, which also has a set of tenses, but used in very different, and specific, circumstances. One of these, in the present tense, is used, as you saw in the dialogue, after the verb *to hope*, or *to wish*, when you are wishing something for someone else.

It is also used after the following, amongst many others:

esperar que	*to hope/wish that*
duvidar que	*to doubt that*
sentir que	*to feel sorry that*
é impossível que	*it is impossible that*
é incrível que	*it is incredible that*
é improvável que	*it is improbable that*

The main trigger is the word **que**, as it is the verb which follows **que** that goes into the subjunctive form. You have in fact come across the subjunctive before, in the guise of commands. Remember in Unit 7, you learnt how the endings of **-ar** verbs became like **-er** verbs, and those of **-er** and **-ir** verbs became like **-ar** ones? That is the formation of the present subjunctive. Here again to remind you are our three regular verbs:

Present		subjunctive	
falar to speak	**fale**	**fale**	**falemos**	**falem**
comer to eat	**coma**	**coma**	**comamos**	**comam**
partir to depart/leave/break	**parta**	**parta**	**partamos**	**partam**

Look at these examples:

Espero que você coma bem.	*I hope that you eat well.*
Ela duvida que ele parta amanhã.	*She doubts that he will depart tomorrow.*
É impossível que elas escrevam tanto.	*It's impossible that they (should) write so much.*

As usual, watch out for irregulars.

The subjunctive is something that takes a long time to sink in, but at least with a small notion of it under your belt, you are armed to understand a little bit more about the structures that may be used in conversation with you.

Dialogue 3

On the way back home Marli witnesses an accident. She goes over to the injured person.

CD2, TR 8: 02:37

Marli	Você precisa de ajuda?
Sr	Obrigado. Tenho uma dor na perna. Acho que está partida. Que dor! Não posso mexer nada.
Marli	Que aconteceu?
Sr	Eu estava atravessando a rua sem problemas; tinha chegado mais ou menos ao centro quando de repente – baf! – um carro me bateu e aqui estou.
Marli	Parece que o carro não parou. Idiota! Bom, não se preocupe, senhor. Vou chamar uma ambulância. Não demora muito.

	(Marli uses the telephone in a nearby shop.)
Marli	Alô, escute, houve um acidente na rua Moraes Sales.
Telefonista	Tem alguém ferido?
Marli	Sim, um senhor, a perna foi quebrada quando um carro a bateu. Precisamos duma ambulância.
Telefonista	Onde está exatamente?
Marli	Na rua Moraes Sales perto da praça Paulista, ao lado da igreja Santa Augusta. O nome do senhor é Paulo Mendonça.
Telefonista	E seu nome senhora?
Marli	Eu sou Marli Ferreira.
Telefonista	Está bem. Uma ambulância está a caminho.

ajuda (a) *help*
mexer *to move*
que aconteceu? *what happened?*
estava atravessando *was crossing*
tinha chegado *had arrived*
de repente *suddenly*
bateu *hit*
quebrada, partida *broken*
parou *stopped*
idiota (o) *idiot*
demora *take a while*
escute *listen*
ferido *injured*
foi quebrada *was broken*
está a caminho *is on the way*

QUICK VOCAB

Grammar

Imperfect

In Unit 14 you saw how you could use the verb **estar** plus the gerund – the 'ing' part of the verb (**-ando/-endo/-indo**) – to make an action that is currently happening. You can also do this using the imperfect of **estar** and the gerund to describe an action in the past which was in the process of happening, e.g. **Estava atravessando** *I was crossing*. This is used more commonly than the pure imperfect on its own – **atravessava** *I was crossing*.

The past, part 3

If you want to describe an action which took place and was completed before another past action began, you use a tense known as the pluperfect. In English it corresponds to *had done*. Look at these examples in English:

When he arrived home, she had (already) gone out.
We were sure he had told us a lie.

And from the dialogue:

Tinha chegado ... quando de repente ...	*I had arrived ... when suddenly ....*

This tense is often used in relating incidents, or giving a report of a sequence of events.

It is formed using the imperfect of **ter**, plus the past participle. For example:

Eles tinham comido muito.	*They had eaten a lot.*
Maria tinha falado com ele antes de sair.	*Maria had spoken with him before going out.*

The passive

With most actions, there are two ways of expressing what has happened. Look at these two examples:

1 Paulo quebrou a perna. *Paul broke his leg.*
2 A perna foi quebrada (por ...) *The leg was broken (by ...).*

Statement 1 is known as an active sentence, where the subject of the verb actively carries out the action. Statement 2 is called a *passive sentence*, because the object in fact becomes the subject, or is acted upon by someone or something, known as the agent.

The passive is constructed using **ser** plus the past participle of the relevant verb, used as an adjective. If you want to say who or what the agent was/is, you introduce it with **por** by. For example:

A janela foi fechada pela professora.	*The window was closed by the teacher.*
Os soldados foram mortos.	*The soldiers were killed.*
Eu fui mordido por uma abelha.	*I was stung by a bee.*

estar and the past participle used as an adjective conveys the *state* something is in as a result of an action, e.g.

A janela estava fechada.	*The window was closed (i.e. We can see it has already been closed.).*
Ele estava perdido.	*He was lost.*

Practice

1 Can you now:
    a Say that you don't feel at all well.
    b Ask your husband/wife where it hurts.
    c Ask if the chemist has anything for toothache.
    d Ask what he has for migraines.
    e Ask what has happened.
    f Tell the emergency services that there's been an accident on Campo street.

2 Link up the statements on the next page with the pictures below.

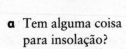

a Tem alguma coisa
para insolação?

b Dói-me a barriga.

c João bateu o dedo.

d Ele tem uma dor nos
olhos.

e Meu marido tem uma dor
de cabeça.

f Cortei a perna. Preciso
de um band-aid.

3 Link up the two parts of each sentence correctly, and form the
second verb (in brackets) in the subjunctive.

a Esperamos que	**i**	eles [estudar] tanto.
b Sinto muito que	**ii**	nós [ganhar] muito dinheiro.
c É incrível que	**iii**	sua filha [melhorar].
d Ela duvida que	**iv**	Sonia [estar] doente.
e É impossível que	**v**	ele me [amar].
f Espero que	**vi**	ele [vir] hoje.

◆》 **CD2, TR 8, 04:19**

4 Listen to the phone call to the emergency services and write
down the following information.

Accident where?	How many	Injuries?	Exact
Name of caller?	injured?		location?

5 Place the correct past form of the verb and give any other information required to complete the sentences.

  a A escola **ser/estar** _____ [*closed*] _____ durante as férias.

  b Os presentes **ser/estar** _____ [*given*] _____ aos turistas [*by the hotel owner*] _____ _____.

  c As portas **ser/estar** _____ [*open*] _____.

  d Eu **ser/estar** _____ [*invited*] _____.

  e A carta **ser/estar** _____ [*written*] _____ [*by Luís*] _____ _____.

  f Os sapatos **ser/estar** _____ muito [*dirty*] _____.

6 Complete your part of the dialogue at the chemist's.

You	(*Ask the pharmacist do you have anything for a headache?*)
Farm.	Sim, temos estas aspirinas que são boas, ou tem estes comprimidos.
You	(*Say I'll take the aspirins.*)
Farm.	É só?
You	(*Say no, what do you have for allergies?*)
Farm.	Tem este creme repelente, se é alergia a insetos, ou estes comprimidos antihistamínicos.
You	(*Say I'll take a bottle of the cream. How much is that please?*)
Farm.	São 6 reais e 40 centavos, por favor.
You	(*Say thank you and goodbye.*)

Insight

It's advisable to have any injections before you get to Brazil, drink only bottled water and avoid any shellfish, which may not be freshly caught. Chemists can be extremely helpful; hospital treatment is chaotic, although there is an excellent hospital in São Paulo. Most medication is available, but take supplies if you are travelling inland or into the Amazon.

Dialogue 4

It's time for Sylvia to leave. The Ferreiras have taken her to the airport and are saying goodbye.

CD2, TR 8, 05:03

José Sylvia, foi tão bom te ver outra vez. Volte logo – sabe que tem uma casa aqui sempre. Será sempre bem-vinda.

Sylvia Obrigada, José. E Marli também, obrigada por tudo. Foi uma visita fantástica, e vocês foram muito generosos. Espero-os lá na Inglaterra, tá? A próxima vez vocês vão ficar conosco.

Marli Foi um prazer te conhecer finalmente. José tinha falado tanto em ti. Volte sempre, e nossos cumprimentos ao resto da família. Leve consigo estes CDs da nossa música.

Sylvia Que legal! Gilberto Gil, Milton Nascimento, Simone, alguns dos meus músicos preferidos. Obrigada e até à próxima.

José Se Deus quiser.

Sylvia E se eu ganhar na loteria! Adeus. Tchau, tchau!

QUICK VOCAB

volte logo *come back soon*
por tudo *for everything*
generosos *kind*
foi um prazer *it was a pleasure*
finalmente *finally*
em ti *about you*
músicos preferidos (os) *favourite singers*
se Deus quiser *hopefully/God willing*
se eu ganhar na loteria *If I win the lottery*
volte sempre *come back again*

Test yourself

não me sinto nada bem	*I don't feel at all well*
o que você tem?	*what's the matter (with you)?*

me dói/doem	*my ... hurt/s*
não se preocupe	*don't worry*
tem alguma coisa para ...?	*do you have anything for ...?*
o que tem para ...?	*what do you have for ...?*
espero que melhore	*I hope you get better*
que aconteceu?	*what (has) happened?*
houve um acidente	*there's been an accident*
volte sempre	*come back (again)*

Congratulations on completing *Complete Brazilian Portuguese!*

I hope you have enjoyed working your way through the course.
I am always keen to receive feedback from people who have
used my course, so why not contact me and let me know your
reactions? I'll be particularly pleased to receive your praise, but
I should also like to know if you think things could be improved.
I always welcome comments and suggestions and I do my best to
incorporate constructive suggestions into later editions.

You can contact me through the publishers at:
Teach Yourself Books, Hodder Headline Ltd, 338 Euston Road,
London NW1 3BH.

I hope you will want to build on your knowledge of Portuguese
and have made a few suggestions to help you do this in the section
entitled **Taking it further**.

Boa sorte, e força!
Sue Tyson-Ward

Testing yourself: Units 1–9

In this unit you will have further practice on the grammatical points and vocabulary items from Units 1–9. You may wish to revise the Grammar sections before you begin, or use this unit as a progress test. All the answers are in the Key to Testing yourself.

1 Decide which article is required for each noun, and tick the appropriate boxes.

	o	a	os	as
livro				
casa				
filhas				
prato				
jornais				
	um	**uma**	**uns**	**umas**
cidade				
senhores				
ruas				
país				
estação				

2 Supply the correct form of the demonstrative (**este** or **aquele**, etc.) in each case.

    a _____ livro que tenho é francês.

    b _____ hotéis ali na praça são muito bons.

    c Gosta d _____ casas aqui?

    d _____ senhora é minha amiga.

3 Use the correct form of **todo** (**tudo**) etc.

    a _____ é muito interessante aqui.

    b _____ minhas amigas estudam português.

    c Ela não gosta de _____ o filme.

    e Quero comprar _____ a roupa.

f Nós adoramos _____ neste país.

g _____ as semanas vou ao cinema.

4 Write out the Portuguese for these numbers.

a 36	**f** 12,654
b 152	**g** 25,999
c 500	**h** 100,000
d 1,321	**i** 14
e 5,800	**j** 95

5 What are these numbers?

a oitocentos e noventa e nove

b setecentos e vinte e três

c quatrocentos e sessenta e oito

d dois mil, quinhentos e um

e quatro mil, oitocentos e dois

f sete mil, quinhentos e cinquenta e quatro

g onze mil e cem

h sessenta e oito mil, trezentos e trinta e seis

i cento e cinco

j trezentos e sete

6 Form the present tense correctly.

a Eles não [comer] _____ carne.

b Eu [falar] _____ alemão.

c Você [ir] _____ ao trabalho?

d Ela não [partir] _____ hoje.

e Nós [fazer] _____ muito barulho.

f João [viajar] _____ todos os meses.

g Vocês não [escrever] _____ muitas cartas.

h Os senhores [compreender] _____?

7 Decide in each case whether the verb should be **ser**, **estar** or **ficar**, and write the correct form.

a Ela [ ] francesa.

b Onde [ ] minha bolsa?

c O banco [ ] ao lado do museu.

d As chaves [ ] em cima da mesa.

    e Todas as lojas [   ] muito perto do centro.
    f Eles [   ] engenheiros.
    g O apartamento [   ] no segundo andar.
    h João [   ] meu amigo.

8 Make up whole sentences by selecting an appropriate form of
ter or **haver** and using a suitable ending.

a	Meu irmão	temos	**i**	um bom carro.
b	Na cidade	têm	**ii**	quinze anos.
c	Nós	tem	**iii**	para beber?
d	O que	há	**iv**	meu livro?
e	Não	tem	**v**	muitas pessoas.
f	Júlia e Maria	há	**vi**	fome.
g	Você	tenho	**vii**	lojas interessantes.
h	Na praça	há	**viii**	uma casa grande.

In the Key you will find suggested sample answers.

9 Form the correct part of the command in each phrase.
    a Falar [sing.] mais devagar.
    b Comer [sing.] menos.
    c Fechar [sing.] a porta.
    d Não abrir [plur.] as janelas.
    e Beber [plur.] mais água.
    f Não subir [plur.] estas escadas.
    g Começar [sing.] agora.
    h Preencher [sing.] esta ficha.

10 Follow the clues to fill in the crossword on nationalities and
countries.
    Across: 1 Pessoas dos Estados Unidos.
               2 O país dos ingleses.
               3 A língua dos espanhois.
               4 Rio é no ...
    Down: 5 Paris é o capital da ...
               6 Vêm da Alemanha.
               7 Da Grécia.

8 País dos italianos.
9 Pessoa da China.
10 Os alemães vêm da …

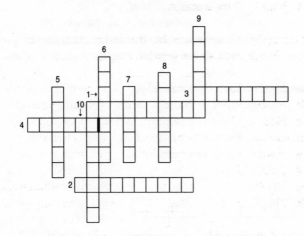

11 Can you complete these words, which are all items of clothing?

a v------
b s---
c c--ç-

d --p-t-
e --m-a
f b-u--

g -h---u
h l-v--
i c-s---
j g----t-

12 Can you find nine colours in this wordsearch?

V	E	R	M	E	L	H	O
E	O	O	T	P	A	M	C
R	L	X	B	C	O	D	N
D	E	O	P	R	E	F	A
E	R	F	R	G	O	H	R
A	A	A	E	B	C	S	B
A	M	Z	T	L	U	Z	A
Q	A	N	O	J	P	T	W

13 Follow the clues and complete the crossword on shops and facilities.

Across:
1 Grande loja.
2 Para trocar dinheiro …
6 Onde se compram botas, sapatos, etc.
7 Onde se vendem frutas, legumes, peixe …
8 Fica na rua – para comprar jornais, mapas, revistas.

Down:
3 Para comprar selos …
4 Onde se compra carne.
5 Onde se compram livros.
9 Para comer e beber …
10 Onde se vê um filme.

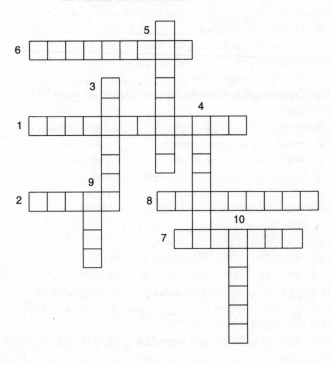

Testing yourself: Units 10–18

In this unit you will have further practice on the grammatical points and vocabulary items from Units 10–18. You may wish to revise the Grammar sections before you begin, or use this unit as a progress test. All the answers are in the Key to Testing yourself on Units 10–18.

1 Form adverbs from the words in brackets.
   a [súbito] _____ vi meu amigo na praça.
   b [final] _____ os alunos terminaram o exame.
   c Sai daqui [imediato] _____!
   d Não entendo esta língua [fácil] _____.
   e [aparente] _____, ela só tem treze anos!
   f Ela está [temporário] _____ fora do país.
   g Os dois irmãos cantam muito [mau] _____.

2 Change the verbs from the present tense to the preterite.
   a Elas não [compreendem] _____ muito.
   b Todos os trenes [partem] _____ tarde.
   c Eu [vendo] _____ fotografias.
   d Maria e Sônia [chegam] _____ de táxi.
   e Pedro [está] _____ no hospital.
   f Vocês [percebem] _____ tudo?
   g Você [tem] _____ dinheiro?
   h [tiramos] _____ as malas do hotel.

3 Form the imperfect tense correctly in these examples.
   a Quantos anos [ter] _____ você quando foi para a Alemanha?
   b Durante as férias nós [acordar] _____ tarde todos os dias.
   c Eu [estar] _____ tomando banho quando ele telefonou.

d Eles [sentir-se] _____ cansados depois de trabalhar todo o dia.

e Ela só [querer] _____ comprar uma coisa – uma blusa amarela!

f Antigamente, ele [ir] _____ ao cinema cada semana.

4 Choose the correct form of **ter**, and form the past participle of the verbs in bold, to form sentences using the pluperfect tense.

a Maria e Lû	tinha	**ir** ao cinema quando eu cheguei.
b Eu	tinha	**comprar** um novo carro.
c O professor	tinha	**falar** muito antes de terminar
	tinham	a aula.
d Eu e José	tínhamos	**comer** pouco.
e Sra Guedes	tinham	**subir** ao quarto quando o
		marido telefonou.
f Vocês		**viver** na França.

5 Change the verbs in **bold** into the present subjunctive.

a Espero que você **ter** uma boa viagem.

b Ana quer que o filho **estudar** bem.

c Talvez ela **fazer** um bolo delicioso.

d Duvidamos que vocês **abrir** seus livros hoje.

e É estranho que eles não **ir** à escola.

f Talvez nós não **falar** muito bem.

6 Write the answers to these sums in full in Portuguese.

a 53 + 72 = _____

b 14 + 9 = _____

c 180 – 25 = _____

d 250 ÷ 5 = _____

e 46 + 362 = _____

f 841 + 659 = _____

g 1200 ÷ 20 = _____

h 5 × 500 = _____

i 25,364 – 63 = _____

j 123,801 + 99 = _____

7 Are the following numbers written correctly in Portuguese? If they are not, give the correct form in full.

		✓/✗	correct version
a	531 = quinhentos e trinta e um	☐	_____
b	1,250 = mil, duzentos e cinquenta	☐	_____
c	348 = trezentos e quarenta e nove	☐	_____
d	96 = noventa e seis	☐	_____
e	5,221 = cinco mil, duzentos e	☐	_____
	trinta e um	☐	_____
f	26,860 = vinte e seis mil,	☐	_____
	novecentos e sessenta	☐	_____
g	72 = setenta e dois	☐	_____
h	28 = vinte e oito	☐	_____

8 Choose the appropriate past participle from the box for each sentence to form a passive. Make it agree with the noun/pronoun.

a O gato foi _____ pelo cão.

b A porta foi _____.

c Eles foram _____ pelos soldados.

d O carro foi _____.

e As casas foram _____ pelo terremoto (*earthquake*).

f Eu (fem.) fui _____.

> morto
> decepcionado
> vendido
> mordido
> destruído
> aberto

9 Can you find ten items of food or drink in this wordsearch?

O	B	M	E	Y	O	K	G	S	L
T	S	A	N	D	U	Í	C	H	E
N	O	L	E	I	T	E	Y	O	G
U	P	J	F	A	R	U	P	J	U
S	A	C	N	V	M	Ã	C	N	M
E	Y	O	E	Y	O	K	G	S	E
R	O	J	I	E	U	Q	R	U	S
P	A	Ç	Ú	C	A	R	U	P	J
F	A	C	N	W	T	I	L	H	D
Z	V	M	Q	R	O	H	N	I	V

10 Follow the numerical guidance, and fill in ten months of the year on the grid.

Across: 1 o décimo-primeiro mês
2 o quinto mês
3 o segundo
4 o quarto
5 o décimo-segundo
6 o sétimo

Down: 7 o primeiro mês
8 o nono mês
9 o terceiro
10 décimo

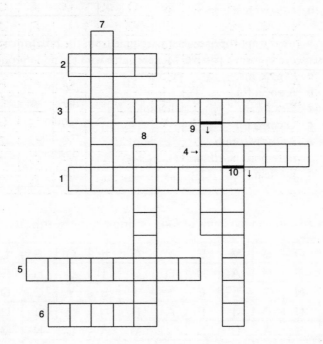

11 Find the opposite pairs.

a	alto	**i**	magro
b	gordo	**ii**	chato
c	velho	**iii**	feio
d	interessante	**iv**	horrível
e	simpático	**v**	baixo
f	bonito	**vi**	jovem

12 Can you find ten parts of the body in this wordsearch?

O	L	H	O	K	G	S	M	Ã	O
K	G	S	X	B	Q	R	U	P	J
F	A	C	N	Q	D	O	K	G	S
X	B	C	A	B	E	Ç	A	C	N
A	C	N	O	K	D	A	C	N	P
N	W	C	N	R	O	R	U	P	É
R	A	C	N	W	E	B	Q	R	U
E	Y	R	U	P	J	L	H	D	Z
P	J	F	I	L	H	D	H	D	Z
V	M	E	Y	Z	V	M	E	A	C

Taking it further

A selection of information on further reading, websites, and things connected with Brazilian Portuguese.

Reading

História da língua portuguesa, Paul Teyssier (Sá da Costa, 1990)
The Romance Languages, Martin Harris and Nigel Vincent (Routledge, 1997)
The Loom of Language, Frederick Bodmer (Allen & Unwin, 1946)
Dicionário Editora da língua portuguesa, good monolingual dictionary (new edn 1994)
Oxford–Duden Pictorial Dictionary, detail visual/vocabulary (1992)
Michaelis dicionário práctico, bilingual (English–Portuguese, both directions)
Collins Portuguese dictionaries, various sizes
In Action CD-ROM (Brazilian), Linguaphone
Brazil: The Once and Future Country, M.C. Eakin (St Martin's, 1997)
Lonely Planet Brazilian Phrase Book, M. Balla (Lonely Planet, 1990)
Books by Paulo Coelho, in English or the original
Heliopolis (novel), James Scudamore (Harvill Secker, 2009)
A Death in Brazil (A book of omissions), Peter Robb (Bloomsbury, 2005)
Two magazines available in the UK designed for the Brazilian community, both have useful contacts and reading material:
REAL: Tel: 020-8534-6183, or online: www.revistareal.com
LEROS: email: leros@leros.co.uk, or online: www.leros.co.uk

Learning

BBC series *Talk Portuguese*, 2003, includes one programme in Brazil. Also, *Brazil Inside Out*, 2003, a five-programme documentary series, with interviews with local people in five Brazilian regions.

Satellite TV, if you have access to it, will be able to reach Portuguese TV; there is an international channel called RTPi, which often features Brazilian telenovelas, or soap operas.

On-line courses, such as that offered by the University of Glasgow (UK), called *De tudo um pouco*.

Various Portuguese-learning CD-ROMs now available from good bookstores.

Enrol on language classes at your local college/language school.

Try to speak to Brazilians when you are in Brazil – they will be grateful you have made an effort, and will encourage your attempts.

Websites

There are many sites and materials in both English and Portuguese. Here are just a few ideas:

Brazil on the web (Brazilian Embassy site): www.brazil.org.uk

Comunidade de Países de Língua Portuguesa – Portuguese-speaking communities: www.cplp.org

King's College, London – Dept. of Portuguese and Brazilian studies, various links: www.Kcl.ac.uk/depsta/humanities/pobrst/kclhp.htm

Língua Portuguesa – key this into any search engine (Altavista, Google, etc.) and you should link to many more sites.

Grant & Cutler – stockists of Portuguese books in the UK: www.grant-c.demon.co.uk

Universidade de S. Paulo: http://www.usp.br

Art and culture: www.insite.com.br/art

Veja magazine: www.veja.com.br

Brazilian cinema: www.cinemabrasil.org.br

Brazilian Consulate in the UK: www.consbraslondres.com

Brazilian TV channel: www.tvglobointernacional.com.br

Casa do Brasil em Londres – all kinds of services, including translations: www.casadobrasil.org.uk

Key to the exercises

Unit 1

True or false? a F b F c V

Exercise 1 1 b 2 b 3 a

Exercise 2 a Boa, Bem, b é c muito

Practice 1 a bom dia/boa tarde/boa noite (tarde) b obrigado/a, tchau c sou/meu nome é X d Tem um apartamento reservado em meu nome? e Oi, tudo bem? 2 Aqui está. / Sim, sou. / Oito dias. / Tchau (adeus) 3 a sete b catorze c dezessete d onze e treze 4 i dezoito 18 ii dez 10 5 a ii b iv c i d iii e v 6 a John Harris b Liverpool c 6 days d room 12

Testing yourself – do you understand? 1 male 2 false 3 true 4 en-suite (5) false

Unit 2

True or false 1? a f b f c v d f e v

True or false 2? a f b f c v

Practice 1 Não, sou de Birmingham. / É grande e industrial. / Sim, tenho um filho. / Ele se chama David. Tem 28 anos e é professor de francês. / Sim, trabalho numa empresa internacional. 2 a iii b v c i d ii e iv 3 1 a 2 b 3 b 4 4 a cinco/pequenas b brasileira c filhos interessantes d histórica e dois vinhos alemães

Testing yourself – do you understand? 1 22 years old 2 very big, modern, very interesting, 3 no 4 language student, school secretary 5 Olá, John, Tudo bem? Eu estou muito bem. Vou te dizer um pouco sobre quem sou. Meu nome é Gary, tenho vinte e cinco anos e sou de Bristol. É uma cidade muito bonita – histórica, e turística. Sou casado e tenho um filho, Robert. Sou estudante de tecnologia. Tchau, Gary.

Unit 3

True or false? a f b v c v d v e f

Exercise a sim b não c não

Practice 1 a é b são c está d é e sou/sou 2 Não, sou de Brighton. / É uma cidade pequena ao sul de Inglaterra. / Sim é bastante perto. 3 a i b ii c ii d iii e iii 4 1 Santos 2 Cantanduva 3 Campinas 4 Piracicaba 5 Uberaba

Testing yourself – do you understand? 1 f 2 f 3 v 4 f

Unit 4

Exercise 1 a no b yes c no

True or false? a v b f c f

Exercise 2 1 b 2 a 3 a

Practice 1 a Há/tem um açougue por aqui? b Onde há/tem um correio? c Que horas são? d São 2 e meia. e Na Alemanha chove (um) pouco. 2 a iii b i c iv d ii e v 3 a farmácia b mercado c café Silvana d praça D. Pedro 4 a Mexico b Japan c Brazil d France e England 5 Desculpe, sabe se há/tem um mercado por aqui? / Sabe se está aberto agora? / São dez e um quarto (quinze). / Fica longe? / Obrigado/a, adeus (tchau). 6 a fica b ali c aqueles d terceira e para

Testing yourself – do you understand? 1 post office 2 Gomes Sá Street 3 Nascimento Street 4 4pm. 5 no

Unit 5

Exercise 1 a grande b num café c muito

Exercise 2 a f b v c f

Practice 1 a saio de casa b começo o trabalho c 12.45 d 1.30 e 18.05 2 a às sete e meia b às quinze para às nove c às duas e meia d às quatro e 25 e à uma e quinze f às dez para às oito 3 a Portugal é a seiscentos km da França. b O Brasil é a mil, oitocentos e noventa e seis km do México. c A Inglaterra é a mil, duzentos e quarenta e sete km de Portugal. d Os Estados Unidos são a seis mil, cento e vinte e cinco km da Argentina. 4 a iii b i c v d ii e iv

Testing yourself – do you understand? 1 true 2 Portuguese 3 D 4 A 5 false 6 E – airport

Unit 6

Exercise a sports/TV b sports/TV c reading/music

True or false? a v b f c v

Practice 1 a ii b v c i d iv e iii 2 a conheço b sabe c sei d conhece e conhecem 3 Speaker 1=C, 2=A, 3=B 4 Adoro nadar, vou à piscina aos sábados. / Sim, um pouco. / Prefiro a música jazz. Francisco, o que você faz no tempo livre? / Também gosto do teatro, mas os ingressos são bastante caros.

Testing yourself – do you understand? 1 Vinhos / Mary Black / High Street, no. 10 / CEP 23410 Centro / Southampton Hants. 2 a violão b mecânica geral c desenho artístico e publicitário

Unit 7

Exercise 1 C

Exercise 2 a sapatos b 39 c R85

Practice 1 a ii b iii c i d vi e v
2 Tem saias? / Acho que é o 42. / Tem em azul-claro? / Quanto
é, (custa)? / Levo esta em azul e aquela em preto. / Obrigada
3 a compre / Buy the blouse! b comam / Eat the bread! c vão / Go
through (by) here! d faça / Don't be noisy! e trabalhe / Work hard!
f falem / Don't talk a lot! 4 a boots b 39 c brown d too big e R$98

Testing yourself – do you understand? 1 salads 2 eat fruits, not
sweet things, 3 make a dinner 4 have a good salt bath 5 relax a lot
6 massage

Unit 8

Exercise 1 a v b f c f

Exercise 2 a yes b no c yes

Practice 1 a Tem uma mesa livre? b Somos cinco. c Não tenho
sede. d Que vai pedir? e Garçom por favor. f A conta por favor.
2 a sigam b faça c beba d repitam e falem f traga 3 Para começar
uma sopa de legumes. / Ovelha com arroz e salada. / Uma cerveja e
uma jarra de água. 4 sobremesa / hoje / sorvete / baunilha / avelã /
sim 5 a tenho fome b tem calor c temos sono d tem frio e têm sede
6 a iii b ii c i d iv 7 a dessert b drink c drink d starter e main meal
f side dish g starter h side dish

Testing yourself – do you understand? Laura – creme de aspargos,
omelete, fruta. Marcelo – canja, frango, doce de côco. Sérgio – lula
frita, espeto misto, pudim de caramelo. You – no starter, bife na
brasa, sorvete. Rita – canja, peixe, fruta.

Unit 9

Practice 1 a meus b sua/ a amiga dele c nossa d suas/ as irmãs delas
e sua 2 a Pode me levar ao centro da cidade? b Boa viagem!
c A que horas parte o próximo ônibus (de luxo) para o Rio?

d Tem troco para uma nota de R$50? e O que faço para chegar na praça Miraflores? f Conhece um bom restaurante aqui? 3 A que horas parte o próximo ônibus para Fortaleza? / Queria um bilhete de ida e volta. / Tem troco para uma nota de R$100? / O ônibus sai de onde? 4 a iv b i c v d iii e ii 5 c/f/a/d/g/b/e/h

Testing yourself – do you understand? 1 T 2 F 3 F

Unit 10

Exercise 1 a R$360 b no c no

Exercise 2 Any 3 of: air-conditioning not working / tap won't close / pillow dirty / blinds don't open properly

Practice 1 Bom dia, tem um apartamento livre? / Simples por favor. Com banheiro. / Para três dias. / Quanto é por noite? / (Está bem). Onde fica o apartamento? 2 a iii b i c v d iv e ii or iii f i g i 3 Twin/ with bathroom/3/Saturday/ 135/R$38 per person 4 a Desculpe, o garfo está sujo. b ... o ar-condicionado não está funcionando. c ... a torneira está pingando. d ... o prato está partido. e ... falta uma colher. 5 a ir b comer c terminar d ver e beber

Testing yourself – do you understand? 1 Napoli 2 credit card 3 1 double 4 fridge 5 Silvini 6 38 7 none 8 breakfast and dinner

Unit 11

Practice 1 a odeia a rede b não gosto dos cachimbos c preferimos a cerâmica d gosta dos brincos e adoram os artigos de couro 2 a mim b deles c nela d si e você 3 a 1 b 2 c 1 d 2 e 2 4 Estou procurando presentes para minha família. / Tem uma rede? / Quanto é? / Que tem para senhoras? / Vou levar a rede, e esta tapeçaria.

Testing yourself – do you understand? 1 17 2 from next year 3 40 4 school 5 guaraná and other soft drinks 6 a coelhinho, b quadrinhos, c aulas

Unit 12

Exercise a Aliens b não c satírica d tarde e táxi

Practice 1 a Por que não vamos ao museu? b A que horas começa o filme? c O concerto termina às dez e meia d Que boa exposição! e Você é meu convidado João f Voltamos de ônibus? 2 a eu me b lhe c te d ele e lo 3 a ii b i c ii d Star Wars e 8.30 f i 4 Por que não vamos almoçar naquele barzinho ali? / Venha, eu te convido e sou eu quem pago. / Insisto, você é meu/minha convidado/a. / Vamos. 5 a no avião da b trem das 2 horas c de táxi/a pé d no carro de

Testing yourself – do you understand? a A b B c Vietnam d both e 2 f autobiography

Unit 13

True or false? a f b f c v d f

Practice 1 Boa tarde, quanto custa enviar este pacote a Alemanha por favor? / Bom, queria enviar o pacote e também queria dez selos. / Não, três para Espanha e sete para Inglaterra. / Obrigado/a, onde é a caixa? 2 Buys: ovos / biscoitos / presunto / cerveja / pãezinhos. / Not available: açúcar/mel. / Extra item: olive oil – azeite. 3 a este b essa c aqueles d estes e essas 4 As per CD 5 a Eu posso alugar um carro aqui? b É para oito dias, começando de hoje. c O que faço para chegar no Rio? d Parece que estou perdido/a. e Ponha doze litros de álcool por favor. f Pode verificar a água para mim? 6 a aberto or fechado b abertas or fechadas c feitos d paga e escrita 7 unleaded / 18 litres / no / R$11 8 Bom dia / proibido / praça / perdida / Rio / direita / sinais / segunda / esquerda / estrada

Testing yourself – do you understand? a ii b i c iv d xii e viii f v g ix h vi i x j xi k iii l vii

Unit 14

Practice 1 a Que vai fazer quarta feira à tarde Paul? b Estarei lá
às dez e meia. c Por que não vamos nadar? d A que horas nos
encontramos? e Estou livre a partir das quatro e quinze. f Alô,
quem fala? 2 a Carlos Silves b Banco do Brasil c Thurs a.m. d
French lesson e golf f 11.45 g hospital 3 Examples: a Amanhã eu
comprarei um carro. b O mês que vem nós visitaremos Alemanha.
c No domingo Cristina fará um bolo. d O próximo ano eles
ganharão a loteria. e Depois de amanhã a Sra Lopes escreverá uma
carta. 4 a eles estão dormindo b ela está comendo c nós estamos
estudando d eu estou andando e elas estão falando 5 a f b v c v d
f e f f v 6 a vi b iii c i d ii e iv f v

Testing yourself – do you understand? a novembro b festas c flores
d Estados Unidos e ano f cores 1 nature 2 roses, plants, flowers,
3 new varieties of rose, 15 different colours of petunia 4 1954

Unit 15

Exercise 1 c 2 a 3 b

Practice 1 a Visitou o museu? b Ficamos duas semanas na Itália.
c Quando voltaram de Nova Iorque? d Tem algum recado
para mim? e Acabo de chegar no hotel. f Os italianos falam tão
rapidamente. 2 a comi b compraram c partimos d gostaram e
escreveu 3 a viu b fiz c pusemos d foram e teve 4 Voltei ontem à
tarde. Cheguei aqui às três e vinte e cinco. / Sim, muito. Andei na
praia em Copacabana, visitei o Pão de Açúcar e vi as favelas. / Sim,
comi feijoada e provei a caipirinha. 5 a Eles se levantaram cedo.
b Ela correu rapidamente. c Elas cantaram mal. d Nós falamos
devagar. e Eu toquei piano bem. 6 Inglaterra/ teatro/ visitei/ palácio/
Grécia/ gregos/ interessantes/ dança/ São Paulo/ 5 dias/ Brasília

Testing yourself – do you understand? 1 Estados Unidos.
2 Muito quente. 3 Michael Jackson e atores. 4 Não muito
saudável. 5 Discoteca. 6 Falta de guaraná. 7 sábado.

Unit 16

Exercise a dois quadros b feira-hippy c pedras preciosas

Practice 1 a todas as semanas b todos os anos c todos os ... custam d todos os dias e todas as pessoas ganham f todos os meses 2 Comprei-o (o comprei) na feira-hippy na praça. / Não muito. Só 42 reais. Gosta? / Comprou alguma coisa? / Que livro mais interessante! 3 a carro nosso b estas botas minhas c este gato de José d esta casa sua e estes livros deles 4 1 went to Spain 2 years ago 2 visited Taj Mahal 3 months ago 3 had lunch ½ hour ago 4 went to cinema 5 days ago

Testing yourself – do you understand? 1 umbrella 2 restaurant Mineiro 3 20 minutes ago 4 company name 5 shop doorway

Unit 17

Practice 1 a Havia/tinha uma blusa na vitrine de que gostei. b Estava à direita da vitrine. c Ela era baixa, tinha cabelo comprido e olhos azuis. d Ele tinha provavelmente 40 e tantos anos. e Não é mais interessante hoje em dia? f Nadávamos todos os dias. 2 a fui b era c jantávamos d comiam e veio f estava 3 Body i = dress, long hair ii = t-shirt, skirt, short hair, glasses iii = hat, moustache, shirt, trousers 4 a íamos ii b brincávamos iv c tínhamos i d estudávamos v e passávamos iii 5 Havia/tinha uma camisa na vitrine, mas já não está mais lá. / Era preta e feita de lã. / Estava à esquerda da vitrine detrás das calças. / Não obrigado/a. Só queria aquela. 6 a iii b ii c i d iv

Unit 18

True or false? a v b f c f

Practice 1 a Não me sinto nada bem. b Onde dói? c Tem alguma coisa para dor dos dentes? d (O) que tem para enxaquecas? e Que aconteceu? f Houve/teve um acidente na rua Campo. 2 a iii b iv

c v d vi e ii f i 3 a iii melhore b iv esteja c i estudem d vi venha
e ii ganhemos f v ame 4 D Pedro square / 2 / broken arm, cut leg /
corner with Main Street / Alexandra Esteves 5 a estava fechada
b foram dados pelo dono c estavam abertas d fui convidado/a e foi
escrita por Luís f estavam sujos 6 Tem alguma coisa para dor de
cabeça? / Levo as aspirinas. / Não, que tem para alergias? / Levo
um frasco do creme. Quanto é por favor? Obrigado/a, adeus.

Key to 'testing yourself'

Revision Unit 1

1 o/a/as/o/os uma/uns/umas/um/uma 2 a este b essa c Aqueles
d destas e Esses f Aquela or Esta 3 a Tudo b Todas c todo
d toda e tudo f Todas 4 a trinta e seis b cento e cinquenta e dois
c quinhentos d mil, trezentos e vinte e um e cinco mil e oitocentos
f doze mil, seiscentos e cinquenta e quatro g vinte e cinco mil,
novecentos e noventa e nove h cem mil i catorze j noventa e cinco
5 a 899 b 723 c 468 d 2,501 e 4,802 f 7,554 g 11,100 h 68,336
i 105 j 307 6 a comem b falo c vai d parte e fazemos f viaja
g escrevem h compreendem 7 a é b está c é/fica d estão e são/ficam
f são g é/fica h é 8 a tem ii b há/tem vii c temos viii d há/tem iii
e tenho vi f têm i g tem iv h há/tem v 9 a Fale b coma c Feche
d abram e Bebam f subam g começe h Preencha 10 1 americanos
2 Inglaterra 3 espanhol 4 Brasil 5 França 6 alemães 7 gregos
8 Itália 9 chinês 10 Alemanha 11 a vestido b saia c calças d sapato
e camisa f blusa g chapéu h luvas i casaco j gravata 12 vermelho/
roxo/verde/azul/marrom/rosa/branco/ preto/amarelo 13 Across:
1 supermercado 2 banco 6 sapataria 7 mercado 8 quiosque Down:
3 correio 4 açougue 5 livraria 9 café 10 cinema.

Revision Unit 2

1 a subitamente b Finalmente c Imediatamente d facilmente
e Aparentemente f temporariamente g mal 2 a compreenderam
b partiram c vendi d chegaram e esteve f perceberam g teve
h Tiramos 3 a tinha b acordávamos c estava d sentiam-se e queria
f ia 4 a tinham ido b tinha comprado c tinha falado d tínhamos
comido e tinha subido f tinham vivido 5 a tenha b estude c faça
d abram e vão f falemos 6 a Cento e vinte e cinco b Vinte e três
c Cento e cinquenta e cinco d Cinquenta e Quatrocentos e oito
f Mil e quinhentos g Sessenta h Dois mil e quinhentos i Vinte e cinco
mil, trezentos e um j Cento e vinte e três mil e novecentos

7 a ✔ b ✔ c ✘ trezentos e quarenta e oito d ✔ e ✘ cinco mil,
duzentos e vinte e um f ✘ vinte e seis mil, oitocentos e sessenta
g ✔ h ✔ 8 a mordido b aberta c mortos d vendido e destruídas
f decepcionada 9 sopa/pão/vinho/açúcar/legumes/ sanduíche/
presunto/queijo/ cerveja/leite 10 1 novembro 2 maio 3 fevereiro
4 abril 5 dezembro 6 julho 7 janeiro 8 setembro 9 março
10 outubro 11 a v b i c vi d ii e iv f iii braço/perna/cabeça/mão/
olho/dedo/boca/pé/orelha/nariz

Numbers

um (uma)	1	vinte e um (uma)	21
dois (duas)	2	trinta	30
três	3	quarenta	40
quatro	4	cinquenta	50
cinco	5	sessenta	60
seis	6	setenta	70
sete	7	oitenta	80
oito	8	noventa	90
nove	9	cem (cento)	100
dez	10	cento e um (uma)	101
onze	11	duzentos/as	200
doze	12	trezentos/as	300
treze	13	quatrocentos/as	400
catorze, quatorze	14	quinhentos/as	500
quinze	15	seiscentos/as	600
dezesseis	16	setecentos/as	700
dezessete	17	oitocentos/as	800
dezoito	18	novecentos/as	900
dezenove	19	mil	1 000
vinte	20	um milhão	1 000 000

primeiro/a, 1°/1ª	*first*	sexto/a	*sixth*
segundo/a, 2°/2ª	*second*	sétimo/a	*seventh*
terceiro/a, 3°/3ª	*third*	oitavo/a	*eighth*
quarto/a, 4°/4ª	*fourth*	nono/a	*ninth*
quinto/a, 5°/5ª	*fifth*	décimo/a	*tenth*

BP–English vocabulary

à direita *on the right*
à esquerda *on the left*
a pé *on foot*
abafado *close, hot*
aberto *open*
advogado/a *lawyer*
aeroporto (o) *airport*
agenda (a) *diary*
agora *now*
aguardente (o) *firewater*
álcool (o) *alcohol*
alô *hello*
amigos (os) *friends*
andar (o) *floor*
anos (os) *years*
antigo/a *old*
ao fundo *at the back*
ao lado de *next to*
aos sábados *on Saturdays*
apartamento (o) *room*
aquele/aquela *that*
aqui *here*
arroz com marisco (o) *seafood rice*
às vezes *sometimes*
aspirina (a) *aspirin*
até *until, up to*
avenida (a) *avenue*
avião (o) *aeroplane*
azeite (o) *olive oil*

banco (o) *bank*
banheiro (o) *bathroom*
barco (o) *boat*

barulhento/a *noisy*
bastante *quite*
bem *well*
bem-vindo/a *welcome*
bicicleta (a) *bicycle*
bilhete (o) *ticket*
blusa (a) *blouse*
bolsa (a) *bag*
bom *good, right then*
bonito *pretty*
botas (as) *boots*

cá *here*
cada ... *every ...*
café (o) *café/coffee*
café da manhã (o) *breakfast*
caixa (a) *cash desk, till*
calças (a) *trousers*
cama (a) *bed*
camisa (a) *shirt*
canja (a) *chicken broth*
capoeira (a) *acrobatic dance*
cardápio (o) *menu*
carne (a) *meat*
caro *expensive*
carro (o) *car*
carteira (a) *wallet, purse*
casa (a) *house*
casado/a *married*
casal (o) *couple, double*
cataratas (as) *waterfalls*
cavalo (o) *horse*
cedo *early*
centro (o) *centre*

chamo-me/me chamo
  my name is
chave (a) *key*
chega *arrives*
chope (o) *lager*
chuva (a) *rain*
cidade (a) *town, city*
clube (o) *social club*
coisa (a) *thing*
com *with*
come *s/he eats*
comemos *we eat*
comida (a) *food*
como é? *what is it like?*
comprar *to buy*
comprimido (o) *pill*
conhecer *to get to know*
contra *against*
cor (a) *colour*
correio (o) *post office*
couro (o) *leather*
cultura (a) *culture*
cultural *cultural*
custa *it costs*

daqui *from here*
de nada *don't mention it*
de onde é? *where are you from?*
de onde são? *where are you from?* (pl.)
de vez em quando *sometimes*
debaixo de *underneath*
deixar *to leave*
delicioso/a *delicious*
dentro *inside*
depois *then, after*
desculpe *excuse me*

dia (o) *day*
detrás de *behind*
difícil *difficult*
dinheiro (o) *money*
diz *s/he says*
durante *during*
dúzia (a) *dozen*

e *and*
é *is*
em *in, on*
em frente de *in front of*
em geral *generally*
empresa (a) *business, company*
encher *to fill*
endereço (o) *address*
enorme *enormous*
então *well then*
entre *in between*
escola (a) *school*
escritório (o) *office*
Espanha (a) *Spain*
espanhois *Spanish* (pl.)
esquina (a) *corner*
está bem *OK*
estação (a) *station*
este/esta *this*
estilo (o) *style*
estou bem *I'm well*
estrada (a) *highway*
estudante (o/a) *student*
eu *I*

fala? *do you speak?*
falo *I speak*
família (a) *family*

faça favor de ... please ...
farmácia (a) chemist's
feijoada (a) bean stew
férias (as) holidays
fica is situated
ficar to stay/be situated
ficha (a) form
filha (a) daughter
filho (o) son
flores (as) flowers
fome (a) hunger
fora outside
França (a) France
frango (o) chicken
funcionar to work

garrafa (a) bottle
gasóleo (o) diesel
gasolina (a) petrol
gato (o) cat
gaúcho (o) cowboy
gente (a) people
gentil kind
geralmente generally
gosta/am? do you like?
gostam they like
gostamos we like
gostaria de I would like to
gosto I like
graças a Deus thank goodness
grande big
Grécia (a) Greece

há there is, are
há meia hora ½ hour ago
havia there was, were
histórico historic(al)

hoje today
hotel (o) hotel

ida e volta return (ticket)
ida (a) single (ticket)
idade (a) age
igualmente likewise
incluindo including
índios (os) Indians
informações information
inglês/esa English
internacional international
interessante interesting
ir to go
irmã (a) sister
irmão (o) brother
isso that's it

jacaré (o) alligator, caiman
Japão (o) Japan
jogar to play
jornais (os) newspapers

lá, ali there
lamento I'm sorry
laranjas (as) oranges
leio I read
leite (o) milk
ler to read
levo I'll take
limão (o) lime
limpo clean
lindo pretty
linha (a) platform
litoral coastal
litro (o) litre
livros (os) books

loja (a) shop
Londres London
longe a long way

mãe (a) mother
maior bigger
mais de more than
mais ou menos more or less
mais tarde later
mala (a) suitcase
manteiga (a) butter
mapa (o) map
maravilhoso wonderful
marido (o) husband
mariscos (os) seafood
mas but
médico/a doctor
meio quilo half a kilo
melhorar to improve
mês (o) month
mesa (a) table
mesmo ali right there
moderno modern
momento (o) moment
mora live/s
moram they, you live
moro I live
mosquitos (os) mosquitoes
movimentado busy
muitas vezes often
muito very/much
muito bem very well
muito prazer pleased to
   meet you
mulher (a) wife
mundo (o) world
museu (o) museum
música (a) music

na in/on the
nadar to swim
não no/not
não funciona it doesn't
   work
neve (a) snow
nome (o) name
número (o) number
nunca never

o que faz? what do you do?
obrigado/a thank you
óculos (os) glasses
óleo (o) oil
ônibus (o) bus
ontem yesterday
oportunidade (a)
   opportunity
ouço I listen to
outono (o) Autumn
outros (os) (the) others
ouvir to listen to
ovos (os) eggs

pacote (o) packet
pai (o) father
país (o) country
pais (os) parents
pão (o) bread
para in order to/for
para nós for us
parte departs
partido broken
passamos we spend
passaporte (o) passport
passar to pass/spend
pastelaria (a) cake shop
pedir to ask for

pegar to get, catch
pelo menos at least
pequeno/a small
peras (as) pears
perto near
pessoalmente personally
picante spicy
pingar to drip
pintar to paint
piscina (a) swimming pool
plástico plastic
podem you (pl.) can
podemos we can
pois well
poluição (a) pollution
pôr to put
por noite per night
por favor please
porque because
porta (a) door
porto (o) port
português/esa Portuguese
posso? may I?
postal (o) postcard
pouquinho (um) a little bit
praça (a) square
preciso de I need
preço (o) price
preencher to fill in
prefere he she, you prefer(s)
preferem they, you prefer
preferimos we prefer
prefiro I prefer
presunto (o) smoked ham
primeiro first
problema (o) problem
professor/ora (m/f) teacher
provar to try, taste

provavelmente probably
próximo nearby
puxa! goodness!

quadro (o) picture
qual? which?
quanto é? how much is it?
quantos/as how many?
quarto (o) ¼ litre bottle
quarto (o) bedroom
que that, which
que mais? what else?
que tal? how about?
queijo (o) cheese
quem? who?
quente hot
quer s/he wants
quilo (o) kilo

rápido fast
recepção (a) reception
recomendo I recommend
refeições (as) meals
refeitório (o) canteen
refrigerante (o) soft drink
região (a) region
reservado reserved
reservar to reserve
revistas (as) magazines
roupas (as) clothes
rua (a) road

sabe? do you know?
saia (a) skirt
saída (a) exit
sanduíche (o) sandwich
sapatos (os) shoes
saudável healthy

saúde (a) health
se if
se Deus quiser God willing
selo (o) stamp
sem without
sempre always
senhores (os) you, the gentlemen
sentar-se to sit down
sentir-se to feel
sim yes
sinais (os) road signs
sobremesa (a) dessert
sobrenome (o) surname
somos we are
sorvete (o) ice cream
sou I am
sou de I am from
sujo dirty
suco (o) fruit juice

tamanho (o) size
também also
tão so
tarde (a) afternoon
táxi (o) taxi
tchau bye
telenovelas (as) soap-operas
televisão (a) television
têm they have
tem ...? do you have ...?
temos we have
tempo (o) time
tempo de lazer (o) leisure time
tempo livre (o) free time
tenho I have

terceiro third
terra (a) land, hometown
tipicamente typically
típico typical
todas as noites every night
todos os dias every day
tomar to take
trabalha you work
trabalho I work
transeunte (o) passer-by
trocar to change
tudo everything
tudo bem? OK?

um pouco a bit
um pouco de a bit of
universidade (a) university

vago free
vários/as various
velho/a old
vende s/he sells
vende-se/se vende for sale
vento (o) wind
ver to see, watch
verão (o) summer
vestido (o) dress
viagem (a) journey
vidro (o) window, glass
vinho (o) wine
vir to come
vista (a) view
vive lives

xarope (o) syrup, remedy

English–BP vocabulary

a bit (of) **um pouco (de)**
a long way **longe**
address **endereço (o)**
aeroplane **avião (o)**
afternoon **tarde (a)**
against **contra**
age **idade (a)**
airport **aeroporto (o)**
alcohol **álcool (o)**
alligator **jacaré (o)**
also **também**
always **sempre**
and **e**
arrives **chega**
aspirin **aspirina (a)**
at least **pelo menos**
at the back **ao fundo**
autumn **outono (o)**
avenue **avenida (a)**

bag **bolsa (a)**
bank **banco (o)**
bathroom **banheiro (o)**
bean stew **feijoada (a)**
because **porque**
bed **cama (a)**
bedroom **quarto (o)**
behind **detrás de**
bicycle **bicicleta (a)**
big **grande**
bigger **maior (mais grande)**
blouse **blusa (a)**
boat **barco (o)**

books **livros (os)**
boots **botas (as)**
bottle **garrafa (a)**
bread **pão (o)**
breakfast **café da manhã (o)**
broken **partido**
brother **irmão (o)**
bus **ônibus (o)**
business, company **empresa (a)**
busy **movimentado, ocupado**
but **mas**
butter **manteiga (a)**
bye **tchau**

café/coffee **café (o)**
cake shop **pastelaria (a)**
canteen **cantina (a)**
car **carro, automóvel (o)**
cash desk, till **caixa (a)**
cat **gato (o)**
centre **centro (o)**
cheese **queijo (o)**
chemist's **farmácia (a)**
chicken **frango (o), galinha (a)**
chicken broth **canja (a)**
clean **limpo**
close, hot **abafado**
clothes **roupa (a)**
coastal **litoral**
colour **cor (a)**
corner **esquina (a)**
country **país (o)**
couple, double **casal (o)**

cowboy **gaúcho (o)**
cultural **cultural**
culture **cultura (a)**

daughter **filha (a)**
day **dia (o)**
delicious **delicioso**
departs **parte**
dessert **sobremesa (a)**
diary **agenda (a)**
diesel **gasóleo (o)**
difficult **difícil**
dirty **sujo**
do you know? **sabe?**
do you like? **gosta?**
do you speak? **fala?**
doctor **médico/a (o/a)**
don't mention it **de nada**
door **porta (a)**
dozen **dúzia (a)**
dress **vestido (o)**
during **durante**

early **cedo**
eggs **ovos (os)**
English **inglês**
enormous **enorme**
every **cada**
every day **cada dia/todos os dias**
every night **cada noite/todas as noites**
everything **tudo**
excuse me **desculpe**
exit **saída (a)**
expensive **caro**

family **família (a)**
fast **rápido**

father **pai (o)**
firewater **aguardente (o)**
first **primeiro**
floor **andar (o)**
flowers **flores (as)**
food **comida (a)**
for sale **vende-se**
form **ficha (a)**
France **França (a)**
free time **tempo livre (o)**
friends **amigos (os)**
from here **daqui**
fruit juice **suco (o)**

generally **geralmente**
glasses **óculos (os)**
God willing **se Deus quiser**
good, right then **bom**
goodness! **puxa!**
Greece **Grécia (a)**

half a kilo **meio quilo**
half an hour ago **há meia hora**
health **saúde (a)**
healthy **saudável**
hello **oi**
here **aqui, cá**
highway **estrada (a)**
historic(al) **histórico**
holidays **férias (as)**
horse **cavalo (o)**
hot **quente**
hotel **hotel (o)**
house **casa (a)**
how about? **que tal?**
how many? **quantos?**
how much is it? **quanto é?**

hunger **fome (a)**
husband **marido (o)**

I am from **sou de**
I like **gosto (de)**
I would like to **gostaria (de)**
I'll take **levo**
I'm sorry **lamento/sinto muito**
I'm well **estou bem**
ice-cream **sorvete (o)**
if **se**
in between **entre**
in front of **em frente de**
in order to/for **para**
in, on **em**
in/on the **no, na**
including **incluindo, incluso**
information **informações (as)**
inside **dentro**
interesting **interessante**
international **internacional**
is situated **fica**
it costs **custa**
it doesn't work **não funciona**

Japan **Japão (o)**
journey **viagem (a)**

key **chave (a)**
kilo **quilo (o)**
kind **simpático**

lager **chope (o)**
land, hometown **terra (a)**
later **mais tarde**
lawyer **avogado (o)**
leather **couro (o)**
leisure time **tempo de lazer (o)**

lime **limão (o)/lima (a)**
litre **litro (o)**
live/s **mora**
London **Londres**

magazines **revistas (as)**
map **mapa (o)**
married **casado**
may I? **posso?**
meals **refeições (as)**
menu **cardápio (o)**
milk **leite (o)**
modern **moderno**
moment **momento (o)**
money **dinheiro (o)**
month **mês (o)**
more or less **mais ou menos**
more than **mais (de) que**
mosquitoes **mosquitos (os)**
mother **mãe (a)**
museum **museu (o)**
music **música (a)**
my name is … **o meu nome é …**

name **nome (o)**
near **perto**
never **nunca**
newspapers **jornais (os)**
next to **ao lado de**
no, not **não**
noisy **barulhento**
now **agora**
number **número (o)**

often **muitas vezes**
oil **óleo (o)**
OK **está bem**
old **velho/antigo**

olive oil **azeite (o)**
on foot **a pé**
on Saturdays **aos sábados**
on the left **à esquerda**
on the right **à direita**
open **aberto**
opportunity **oportunidade (a)**
oranges **laranjas (as)**
others **outros/as**
outside **fora**

packet **pacote (o)**
parents **pais (os)**
passer-by **transeunte (o/a)**
passport **passaporte (o)**
pears **peras (as)**
people **gente (a)/pessoas (as)**
per night **por noite**
personally **pessoalmente**
petrol **gasolina (a)**
picture **quadro (o)**
pill **comprimido (o)**
plastic **(de) plástico**
platform **linha (a)**
please **por favor**
pleased to meet you **muito prazer**
pollution **poluição (a)**
port **porto (o)**
Portuguese **português/esa**
post office **correios (os)**
postcard **postal (o)**
pretty **bonito/lindo**
price **preço (o)**
probably **provavelmente**
problem **problema (o)**

quite **bastante**

rain **chuva (a)**
reception **recepção (a)**
region **região (a)**
reserved **reservado**
return (ticket) **ida e volta**
right there **ali mesmo**
road **rua (a)**
road signs **sinais (os)**
room **quarto (o)**

s/he eats **come**
s/he prefers **prefere**
sandwich **sanduíche (o)**
s/he says **diz**
school **escola (a)**
seafood **mariscos (os)**
s/he sells **vende**
shirt **camisa (a)**
shoes **sapatos (os)**
shop **loja (a)**
single (ticket) **ida (a)**
sister **irmã (a)**
size **tamanho (o)**
skirt **saia (a)**
small **pequeno**
smoked ham **presunto (o)**
snow **neve (a)**
so then **então**
soap-operas **telenovelas (as)**
social club **clube (o)**
soft drink **refrigerante (o)**
sometimes **de vez em quando**
son **filho (o)**
Spain **Espanha (a)**
Spanish **espanhol/espanhola**
spicy **picante**
square **praça (a)**

stamp **selo (o)**	to listen to **escutar**
station **estação (a)**	to paint **pintar**
student **estudante (o/a)**	to pass/spend **passar**
style **estilo (o)**	to play **jogar/brincar/tocar**
suitcase **mala (a)**	to put **pôr**
summer **verão (o)**	to reserve **reservar**
surname **sobrenome (o)**	to see, watch **ver**
swimming pool **piscina (a)**	to sit down **sentar-se**
syrup, cough mixture **xarope (o)**	to stay **ficar**
	to swim **nadar**
table **mesa (a)**	to take **tomar/levar**
taxi **táxi (o)**	to try, taste **provar/experimentar**
teacher **professor/a**	to work **trabalhar**
television **televisão (a)**	today **hoje**
thank goodness! **ainda bem!**	town, city **cidade (a)**
thank you **obrigado/a**	trousers **calça (a)**
that **esse/aquele**	typical **típico**
that, which **que**	typically **tipicamente**
then, after **depois**	
there **ali/lá**	underneath **debaixo**
there is, are **há**	university **universidade (a)**
thing **coisa (a)**	until, up to **até**
third **terceiro**	
this **este, esta**	various **vários**
ticket **bilhete (o)**	very **muito**
to ask for **pedir**	very well **muito bem**
to buy **comprar**	view **vista (a)**
to change **trocar/cambiar**	
to come **vir**	wallet, purse **carteira (a)**
to feel **sentir-se**	s/he wants **quer**
to fill **encher**	waterfalls **cataratas (as)**
to fill in **preencher**	welcome **bem-vindo/a**
to get to know **conhecer**	well **bem**
to get, catch **pegar**	well then **então**
to go **ir**	what do you do? **o que faz?**
to improve **melhorar**	what else? **que mais?**
to leave **partir/deixar**	what is it like? **como é?**

where are you from? **de onde é?**
which? **qual?**
who **quem?**
wife **esposa/mulher (a)**
wind **vento (o)**
window **janela (a)**
wine **vinho (o)**
with **com**

without **sem**
wonderful **maravilhoso**
world **mundo (o)**

years **anos (os)**
yes **sim**
yesterday **ontem**
you can **pode**

Grammar index

Numbers refer to units.

Verbs

Grammar